THE

LONG BEACH GAY TRIALS

THE
LONG BEACH
GAY TRIALS

A HISTORY OF INJUSTICE

GERRIE SCHIPSKE

THE
History
PRESS

Published by The History Press
Charleston, SC
www.historypress.com

First published 2025

Manufactured in the United States

ISBN 9781467157711

Library of Congress Control Number: 2024944883

Kudos to Gerrie Schipske for helping shed light on one of the darkest chapters in Long Beach history.

Long Beach has a reputation of being an LGBTQ+-friendly city, but how is that possible when for 102 years, the police department targeted and falsely arrested gay men for lewd conduct?

In her book The Long Beach Gay Trials: A History of Injustice, *Schipske takes readers to when and how it all began in 1914. With comprehensive research, she introduces us to John Amos Lamb, an innocent gay man who was led to slaughter by Long Beach officials who were on a mission to purge the city of "social vagrants" (code for gay men) and maintain traditional values.*

What those officials did to Lamb, and countless other gay men through the decades, was repugnant and un-American.

This book is a must-read for anyone interested in Long Beach history.

—Phillip Zonkel, editor of Q Voice News

CONTENTS

CONTENTS

FOREWORD

G errie Schipske tackles a difficult piece of Long Beach history in her latest book, *The Long Beach Gay Trials: A History of Injustice*. In the 1990s, my law office was overwhelmed with teachers, tax preparers and other ordinary men who happened to be gay and were unlawfully arrested for lewd conduct. This, for behavior that was actually legal. Many lost their jobs and relationships, and some had to register as sex offenders. With other concerned California attorneys—John Duran, Bruce Nickerson, Anthony R.M. Cosio, to name a few—we fought hard. In 2016, the late, great litigator Bruce Nickerson and I attained an unprecedented ruling from courageous Judge Dhanadina that put a halt to these unlawful arrests in Long Beach. I applaud Gerrie for taking an unflinching look at the subject, which ruined lives, so we never have to go back there again.

Audrey Stephanie Loftin, Esq.

ACKNOWLEDGEMENTS

We acknowledge that Long Beach is on the land of the Tongva/ Gabrieleño and the Acjachemen/Juaneño Nations, who have lived and continue to live here. We recognize the Tongva/ Acjachemen Nations and their spiritual connection as the first stewards and the traditional caretakers of this land. We thank them for their strength, perseverance and resistance.

A very special thank-you to my editor, Laurie Krill, whose patience and guidance transformed this book immensely. Also, thank you to both Phillip Zonkel, publisher of *Q Voice News*, who provided a careful review of the book and to attorney and activist Stephanie Loftin, who stood up for the civil rights of gay men being discriminated against by the Long Beach Police Department.

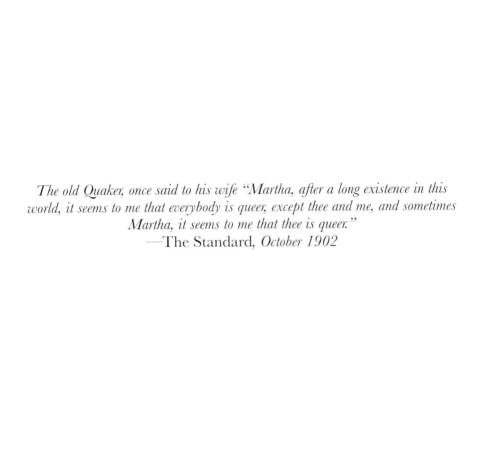

The old Quaker, once said to his wife "Martha, after a long existence in this world, it seems to me that everybody is queer, except thee and me, and sometimes Martha, it seems to me that thee is queer."
—The Standard, *October 1902*

INTRODUCTION

Historical research is like peeling an onion. You start at one level and then open another and another, not quite sure where it will take you. I came upon this story while researching my book *Early Suffragists of Long Beach*. I found that in 1914, Victoria Ellis, the very popular city librarian who had helped with the design of the Long Beach Carnegie Library, was forced to resign because of the political machinations of the newly elected Mayor Louis Napoleon Whealton.

As I read more about Whealton, I found that he conducted secret trials of several city employees. He then took money from the city treasury and in 1914 hired two "special officers" to entrap and arrest "men who made advances to other men" in the public comfort station near the municipal pier. Thirty-one men were arrested and fined $300 to $500, and Whealton was able to pay back the city and make national news.

While reading the many newspaper articles on these arrests, I found that one of those arrested demanded a trial, prompting the *Los Angeles Times* to publish the names of all of the men. One of those listed, John Amos Lamb, killed himself the same day his name appeared. Lamb left a suicide note. Only one of the many newspapers that published the details of his death disclosed the full note, which included the initials of the person Lamb thought was behind what was going on.

Several questions immediately came to mind. Why hadn't the Long Beach newspapers published the arrests, who was John Lamb and who was the "L.H." Lamb named in his suicide note?

I put aside finding the answers while finishing my book on Long Beach suffragists and completed my first attempt at historical fiction in *The Case of the Missing Librarian*, which is about the librarian Whealton drove out.

By chance, I found a reference to the 1914 arrests in *Gay L.A.: A History of Sexual Outlaws, Power Politics & Lipstick Lesbians* by Lillian Faderman and Stuart Timmon (University of California Press, 2006). In the footnotes was a reference to a "Fisher file" containing notes between Long Beach reporter Eugene Irving Fisher and his former employer, C.K. McClatchy, publisher of the *Sacramento Bee*. I was able to obtain a scan of the file from the Center for Sacramento History and found a wealth of insight.

Fisher had to explain to McClatchy just what the "social vagrants" were doing in order to help him understand he was describing homosexual behavior. He knew McClatchy was homophobic and obsessed with a Unitarian minister who had left Sacramento under the rumor of being a "queer." The minister came to Long Beach and set up the first Unitarian church in the city with the help of the ambitious Mayor Whealton and left after being arrested in Santa Monica.

Fisher egged on the homophobic McClatchy to publish details of the "social vagrants" because local newspapers would not. Fisher told McClatchy of his connections with the Los Angeles Police and said that if McClatchy didn't cover these "degenerates," then the Los Angeles papers would. McClatchy responded with a series of articles calling out the immorality in Long Beach.

Fisher fed McClatchy a series of stories of how the men arrested belonged to secret social clubs where they dressed up as women and held orgies. That story was carried nationally, even though there was no proof the clubs existed. The image of the clubs infuriated McClatchy, who was convinced homosexuality was an import from Berlin, Germany, where such clubs existed.

Fisher also pointed out that the current sodomy laws did not include oral copulation and encouraged McClatchy to have his friends in Sacramento change the law. Which he did.

Further research revealed that John Amos Lamb was a sweet, kind man who emigrated from Scotland. Lamb was a pharmacist and owned two successful drugstores in San Bernardino and Long Beach. He moved his mother and sister to Long Beach for his mother's health. He later became a banker. Lamb was very involved in the Episcopal church in San Bernardino and helped found and fund St. Luke's in Long Beach.

I was able to piece together Lamb's social interests from newspaper articles in which he was mentioned. Lamb loved to travel with his sister

Marion, whom he lived with. He loved to sing and did many times with Louis Hazelwood (L.H.) Smith, also a member of St. Luke's vestry and an immigrant. Originally from England, L.H. was a successful realtor in Long Beach and politically connected. Local newspapers printed many stories about social events at which both he and Lamb were listed. For some reason, stories of Lamb and L.H. attending the same events stopped in May 1914 when L.H. received his U.S. citizenship. In August 1914, an article appeared about what a great time L.H. and his brothers had camping on Catalina Island with George Hart, the son of the police judge. A month later, Lamb walked to the city public comfort station, where he was arrested by the two special officers, fined and found guilty by the same police judge.

Two major events pushed me into writing this story.

First was the 2016 trial of a gay man arrested in a Long Beach park restroom. The judge issued a blistering ruling stating that the Long Beach Police Department discriminated against gay men by targeting them in public restrooms. Déjà vu. Unfortunately, several news articles discussed the 1914 arrests and Lamb's suicide inaccurately.

In 2018, I attended the Tom Jacobson play *The Twentieth-Century Way* at the Long Beach Playhouse Studio Theater. The phrase "twentieth-century way" was how reporter Eugene Irving Fisher described oral copulation in his notes to McClatchy. The play is historically inaccurate in its focus on the 1914 arrests, as it characterizes the two special officers as theatrical actors.

It struck me that the complete, accurate story needed to be told about how the political machinations of an ambitious Long Beach mayor and a homophobic newspaper publisher came together to cause the destruction of thirty-one men and the death of John Amos Lamb. No one had told that story.

As the first and only lesbian elected to public office in Long Beach, I felt obligated to tell that story.

—Gerrie Schipske

1

KNOWING THE PRECISE AMOUNT OF POISON

I n 1914, Long Beach could be described as being located about twenty miles from Los Angeles, on the shore of the broad Pacific. Within a short distance lay Terminal Island, a fashionable resort. Farther away, San Pedro became the home of a national seaport. This bustling port and fishing town is the southernmost part of the greater Los Angeles area.

From its earliest days, Long Beach was connected with San Pedro. In 1896, Long Beach resident Iva Tutt owned and operated an electricity plant that generated power produced by a steam engine. She connected Long Beach, San Pedro and Terminal Island by cable and transitioned these towns from kerosene to electric lights.

The Pacific Electric Railroad trolleys further connected the towns by running cars from Long Beach for San Pedro on the half hour from 6:30 a.m. until midnight.

John Amos Lamb knew the precise amount of cyanide of potassium that would kill a man swiftly, surely, yet painfully. The compound is so deadly that it was dispensed and sold only by licensed chemists and pharmacists. Lamb, a chemist and pharmacist by profession, had dispensed the lethal compound many times from his drugstores in San Bernardino and Long Beach. Just one milligram of the white crystalline solid per kilogram of body weight mixed with water would bring almost instant death.

In Lamb's native Scotland, the chemical was first used by the mining industry to extract gold and silver from their ores. Usage quickly expanded to fumigating citrus fruit, developing photographs, cleaning silverware and killing rats.

Those few people who have lived after ingesting the poison by accident report that the solution tastes bitter and cold on the tongue and then creates a burning sensation that produces excessive saliva followed by copious, foaming mucus. A lethal dose can cause the person to become disoriented and suffer convulsions, stiffening of muscles and cardio-respiratory failure in seconds once the solution is swallowed.

In 1914, the law required that should a pharmacist dispense cyanide of potassium, he must know the person to whom he is dispensing the poison and document the date, quantity and the stated purpose for which it will be used.

Because Lamb was so well known in Long Beach, he dared not purchase the poison there. It might delay his plan to trolley to Point Fermin. He could simply convince a pharmacist on duty at the San Pedro Drug Company that

Opening day of Pacific Electric Railway (PE) in 1902. *Author's collection.*

The rocky shore at Point Fermin in 1905. *Public domain. University of Southern California Libraries and California Historical Society.*

he knew the former owner, R.A. Davidson, and that he needed the poison to clean some silverware left by his beloved mother.

He had taken the trolley frequently from his Long Beach home, which he shared with his sister Marion. Lamb and Marion often rode the trolleys to reach Point Fermin, near San Pedro, where they would picnic near breathtaking ocean views.

The weather reported by local newspapers indicates it was a bright, sunny day that November 14, 1914. Tracking back after when Lamb was found, it is clear that he boarded the 7:30 a.m. trolley near his Long Beach home on Broadway and got off at the stop in San Pedro at Beacon and Sixth Street where the San Pedro Drug Company was located. His purchase took only a few minutes. He boarded the trolley again for Port Fermin. The electric car ran to the brink of the cliffs, down which paths lead to the beach below, strewn with huge boulders, battered by incessantly beating surf.

Lamb arrived a little before 9:00 a.m. and walked a short distance to the rocks that line the shore at Port Fermin. The lighthouse station was nearby, at the tip of the peninsula that overlooks both the Los Angeles Harbor to the east and the Pacific Ocean to the south and west. The area was isolated, and few people would be around, especially so early in the morning.

He placed the folded copy of that day's *Los Angeles Times* he had brought with him nearby. He turned it to the front to show his sister's name and the address of the home they shared on Broadway Avenue along the margin. He obviously wanted whoever found him to contact his next of kin and make sure Marion received the note written on a postcard in which he declared his innocence and named L.H.

As a pharmacist, Lamb knew that drinking the poison would cause an almost immediate loss of consciousness and convulsions and that there would be no turning back.

It was done. John Amos Lamb had carried out the execution handed him by two political agents hired by the newly elected, ambitious Long Beach mayor, Louis N. Whealton.

John Lamb was not originally from Long Beach, California. Nor was Mayor Whealton. Actually, few residents of Long Beach were.

Summary of news for November 14, 1914. *From the* Los Angeles Times.

2

WHAT BROUGHT PEOPLE TO LONG BEACH

L ong Beach was known by many names during its earliest period: Rancho Los Alamitos and Los Cerritos, American Colony, Cerritos Colony, Willmore City, the Willows, Queen of the Beaches, Tent City, the Playground of the World, the Home of Industry, Clam City, the National Health Resort and the Wonder City of the Pacific.

After the Spanish seized the land from the Tongva Native people (later known as the Gabrielinos because of their affiliation with the Mission San Gabriel Arcángel), they distributed land grants. In 1784, Spanish governor Pedro Fages granted all the land between the San Gabriel (now also the Los Angeles River) and Santa Ana Rivers to Manuel Nieto for his service as a Spanish solder. The size of the land grant was subsequently reduced by Governor Diego de Borica so as not to infringe on the area occupied by the Mission San Gabriel. Nieto worked the land (referred to as Rancho Los Coyotes), raising cattle, sheep and horses. Up until Nieto's death, the land was divided into five ranchos: Los Coyotes, Los Cerritos, Los Alamitos, Las Bolsas and Santa Gertrudes.

In a succession of real estate transactions, portions of the land within Rancho Los Cerritos owned by John Temple were sold to Flint, Bixby & Company in 1866, and eventually, parts were sold off in lots to settlers and speculators who formed colonies.

The first of these colonies in the Long Beach area was the Cerritos Colony Tract near Willow Street and Pico Avenue. Settled in 1878 by John Teel, it was also the site of the Cerritos school, the first of its kind in the area.

The Southern Pacific Railroad promoted migration to the West Coast in 1869 through the California Immigration Union (CIU), thereby aiming to secure a "good class of foreigners and white Christians from Europe, Canada, and the eastern United States." The government had given the railroads thousands of alternate, odd-numbered sections per mile on each side of the road it no longer needed in order to encourage the expansion of the railroad system across the United States. The railroads also no longer needed the land and were eager to sell.

Long Beach was first called American Colony and then nicknamed Willmore by a newspaper reporter in honor of the man who served as an agent for the railroad and the landowner, California Immigrant Union.

William Erwin Willmore was an educator from England who planned on locating in Pasadena, which was known as a teachers' colony. However, legend says he that when he got off the train near the Pacific Ocean, he was taken back by the expansive marsh set between two rivers, facing the ocean, sheltered by a crescent-shaped beach. Willmore decided to stay.

Cover of booklet marketing the California Immigrant Union. *Library of Congress.*

The CIU was like the others who stole the land from the Indigenous Tongva Gabrielino and exploited it. First, there were the Spanish and then settlers from Maine who had come to California in search of gold but found they could become much richer raising cattle for the miners. Willmore thought he could make his employers even richer in real estate, so he purchased an option on four thousand acres of what was part of the Bixby Ranch. He then hired the state's first civil surveyor, Charles Terraine Healey, who platted out a city that included land for a library, college, residential area, business district and farmland. Restrictive covenants were placed on all land deeds to prevent the selling of liquor.

When freshwater wells were dug and produced ample water for farmland, Willmore and others formed the American Colony Land and Water and Town Association, selling the land at fifty dollars per acre with ten of it placed into a fund for providing water and planting trees.

Willmore, like other agents of the CIU, was hired by white wealthy railroad owners who loathed the Chinese and Mexicans whose labor they exploited. The CIU posted publications that stated its purpose was to attract a population to California:

Belle Lowe, who advocated for Willmore City to be renamed Long Beach. *Author's collection.*

Not of races inferior in natural traits, pagan in religion, ignorant of free institutions and incapable of sharing in them without putting the very existence of those institutions in peril—but we need immigrants of kindred races who will constitute a congenial element and locate themselves and their families permanently upon the soil, who can be admitted to an equal share in our political privileges and respond to all the obligations imposed upon citizens under a republican government.

Despite Willmore's best marketing efforts in newspapers across the country and in Europe, the land did not sell. Willmore eventually went broke and sold the land for $240,000 to Pomeroy and Mills, a group of real estate developers. The business interests quickly set about to rename the colony and agreed with Belle Lowe, the wife of a prominent businessman, who suggested that the town be called after its best asset, its long beach.

From 1884, when Willmore left for Arizona, until 1897, the area changed dramatically. Willmore City became Long Beach. The Long Beach School District, Long Beach High School and the newspaper *Long Beach Journal* were established.

The Long Beach Hotel was built on the bluff, and Judge Maclay Widney provided a steam engine for the transportation to pull a trolley. Because the trolley bogged down on the redwood rails with the weight of passengers, the men got off and pushed it, thereby giving it the name of the "Get Out and Push Railroad."

On January 30, 1888, on a vote of 103–3, male residents approved municipal incorporation and the election of five city trustees. Among the first acts of the city government was to place a tax on dogs and the adoption of an ordinance banning gambling and saloons. The boundaries of the city were expanded.

After Long Beach was incorporated as a city, the railroads decided to expand lines to the area. A newly built pier, bathhouse, swimming tanks, pavilion, auditorium and bowling alley drew thousands of visitors, some of whom stayed and purchased houses and lots or farm acreage.

As saloons were established outside the city boundaries, the residents fought among themselves about whether Long Beach should continue to be a dry city and prohibit the sale of liquor within its boundaries. A vote was taken, and Long Beach was unincorporated in 1896, only to be reincorporated in 1897. The struggle concerning liquor would continue throughout much of the city's early history.

During the fight over liquor, the city remained a largely conservative Methodist community that embraced temperance.

It was the Pacific Electric Railroad (a.k.a. "red cars") that directly connected Los Angeles to Long Beach, which boosted the number of visitors. On its opening day, July 4, 1902, tens of thousands of people

Saloon operated by D.A. McCarty. *Author's collection.*

hopped aboard and celebrated Independence Day in Long Beach, where they enjoyed dancing, swimming, sailing and other festivities. Most importantly, to many who visited or lived there, Long Beach had no saloons and advertised itself as a "dry" city. To others, this presented a problem in attracting visitors.

Long Beach marketed and advertised in 1913 as:

A summer resort just plenty good enough, and it's a place to live the year round with great comfort. There is no use in trying to catalog its attractions. There is a most magnificent stretch of smooth sand for the waves to tumble over. You can gather shells, drive about a country that is one vast park, go fishing, boating, or yachting, try a surf swim or the plunge baths built over the ocean, or idle the hours away on the beach. Long Beach is the summer meeting place of Chautauquan. It is the summer home, too, of thousands of Californians who wish to enjoy an outing amid surroundings moral, educational, and artistic. The city possesses electric lights, a fine pavilion, a city hall, handsome parks, and many new brick business blocks. There will be other people there besides you this summer: over fifteen hundred cottages have been built during the past three seasons. It has a new electric road building…

Long Beach has been long celebrated, earning the title "The Atlantic City of the West." At the landward end of the pier is the great municipal Auditorium, overlooking the crowded Pike and the sweep of the seven-mile strand. Long Beach is a favorite convention city, and many meetings are held in the auditorium. Near the auditorium is the municipal bandstand, where the city's band of forty pieces gives daily concerts. As a residential city Long Beach has been a favorite since its attractiveness became generally known. The population in 1910 was 17,809, increasing from 2,252 in 1900, showing a gain for the decade of 690.8 per cent. The growth since the last census has been little less than phenomenal. The city has many artistic homes, with well-improved gardens and streets. There are five municipal parks. Along the harbor frontage there are many factories, some of them of gigantic proportions. The Craig Shipbuilding Plant has the only shipyard and drydock on the Pacific Coast south of San Francisco. Big vessels, including several for the United States navy have been constructed here. Other important industrial establishments are the Long Beach Salt Works, one of the largest in the West, and the Southern California Edison Company, an immense electrical concern. The Union Oil Company also has a large plant here, and warehouses, lumber yards and factories make up an industrial section which assures a substantial trade for Long Beach in the future. The city also has a growing business section.

Alamitos Beach, adjoining Long Beach on the southeast, is situated on a high bluff overlooking the ocean. Alamitos has a colony of cottages clustered about the pavilion and pier; there is also a small bay here, above which are the Alamitos Heights. The San Gabriel River empties into the ocean at Alamitos Bay, marking the boundary at this point between Los Angeles and Orange counties. Beyond Alamitos is Naples, a growing resort town. Like Venice, this is a place of waterways and canals, connecting the town with Alamitos Bay. There is good boating at this place, with bathing and fishing as added attractions. All along this stretch of coast is splendid accommodation for picnickers. There is a good hotel in Naples and a pavilion patterned after the Palace the Doges at Venice. The resort centers of Bay City, Anaheim Landing and Sunset Beach reach from Naples southward.

By 1910, Long Beach claimed to be "the fastest growing city in the nation" because of the real estate boom that made this seaside resort town a magnet for many sorts. The federal government questioned the city's boasting and sent out an agent to confirm the population count. He reported back positively. Long Beach was growing faster than other cities.

The growth brought new faces to the area. There were those from the East Coast who were lured by the railroads with the promise of cheap land. Midwesterners who came for summer Methodist Chautauqua Bible camps and found this dry city the perfect place to live. Retired Civil War veterans from the North and South sought their fortune in the rich land, which produced feed for cattle and a Mediterranean-type

View of Pine Avenue Pier in 1908. *Library of Congress.*

A 1913 view of the crowded Walk of a Thousand Lights also known as the Pike. *Author's collection.*

climate that nurtured the sweet, citrus fruits that grew in abundance. Aging couples desperate to escape harsh winters and unbreathable city air came to reclaim their health and live their final years in peace and comfort. This group of immigrants earned Long Beach a reputation as the "two graves" city, since a number of cemetery plots were purchased in twos by elderly husbands and wives.

It was the moderate climate and ocean breezes that brought John Amos Lamb to Long Beach in 1902 with his father, his ailing mother and one of his two sisters.

It was the potential to seize power at any cost from a politically unsophisticated growing town that lured Louis Napoleon Whealton to Long Beach in 1908.

3

JOHN AMOS LAMB

PHARMACIST, DEDICATED CHURCHMAN AND BANKER

Life had been especially good to John Amos Lamb and his family since they emigrated from Scotland to California.

John Amos Lamb was born on November 7, 1862. He was given his mother's maiden name as his middle name, which made him feel especially close to her.

The small coal-mining town where he was born, Bathgate, Linlithgowshire, Scotland, held little for the Lamb family. John studied and took his exam to be a member of the Pharmaceutical Society of Great Britain, which allowed him to use the title "Chemist and Druggist."

When his mother became ill and could no longer tolerate the climate of Scotland, John and most of his family, except a brother and one sister, immigrated to the United States in 1887.

The Lambs purchased a farm in San Bernardino County near Rialto in an area that was desert-like and extremely hot during the summers, which was perfect for growing oranges.

John eventually owned and operated several drugstores in downtown San Bernardino with business partners. His most prosperous venture was with Frank Towne, and their store was called Towne & Lamb Drug Store.

He and Towne marketed the store by providing liquid medicines in glass bottles marked with their name and location, which still remain a collector's item to this day. Towne and Lamb were also known for the competitive pricing of their drugs, which they greatly reduced to force other stores to close.

Towne and Lamb Pharmacists marketing bottle. *Worthopedia.com*.

John became a naturalized citizen in 1893 and registered to vote in San Bernardino County in 1898. Voters were required to include a physical description, which was checked when they appeared at the polls. John described himself as "light complexion, gray eyes, brown hair."

By all accounts, John was well respected and liked in his new American community. His drugstore was popular and served as a community meeting place where people gathered for a discussion of politics or a game of checkers.

The store also housed the town's free public library and served as the downtown box office for the very well-attended Kiplinger's Opera House.

In the back of the store stood a contraption built of marble with a pump and spigot where for five cents, the druggist would twirl knobs and manipulate doodads and—with a great amount of fizzing and hissing—produce a more or less cold drink of "sody water." Hence the term *soda fountain*.

Lamb's store also sold ice cream, and its sign could be seen from the dirt road on Third Street in downtown San Bernardino.

John used many gimmicks to attract customers, including the display of a cat he had found in rural San Bernadino. It was advertised as an oddity. The cat had eight legs and two tails, and the local newspapers often mentioned it.

Lamb constantly advertised his drugstore in the local newspapers as "the right place to buy the right drugs at the right price." He offered a mail-order business and free shipping anywhere if more than "$5.03 of drugs were purchased." Because drugs were not manufactured, druggists had to mix and concoct remedies themselves.

John had several passions beyond concocting and selling potions and drugs and sundries. He loved music, playing the piano, singing, writing poetry, traveling and the Episcopal Church.

Although his parents and favorite sister, Marion, were members of the Scottish Presbyterian Church, John was dedicated to the Episcopal Church when he came to the United States.

In San Bernardino, Lamb became actively involved in St. John's Protestant Episcopal Church, serving as choirmaster and donating new chant and service books for Easter. Lamb also spent considerable time on the church vestry and served as its treasurer. When the church burned to the ground in 1887, Lamb helped raise the necessary funds to rebuild. Consequently, he was given the honor of "clerk of the parish" and asked to present the church to Bishop J.H. Johnson at the consecration ceremony—an honor not given to many.

John Lamb's dedication to his church earned him a glowing description by his friends in San Bernardino:

> *A most earnest, conscientious, and devout member of the Protestant Episcopal Church in San Bernardino, being most involved in the activities of the church, particularly in the Sunday school and the vestry. He was a true Christian gentleman, tender and sympathetic in trouble and staunch and firm in his Master's cause. No one ever appealed to him for sympathy or aid in trouble, but they received the help they most needed in full measure.*

John possessed a beautiful voice, and he took it upon himself to volunteer to lead the church choir during a leave of absence of the regular choirmaster. He felt that the laity had a special calling and duty in the church, and by his every action he lived what he taught.

Between his work in the drugstore and the church, Lamb traveled with his sister Marion, taking numerous trips to San Francisco, New York and Long Beach, the seaside town to which he would finally move in 1902 because of his mother's worsening health. Shortly after relocating to Long Beach, his mother fell and hit her chest. She died a few months later.

Marion left San Bernardino to live with John in Long Beach. From the moment she joined him, Long Beach newspapers published accounts of John and Marion entertaining relatives and friends or participating in church events.

Lamb loved Long Beach. He loved the ocean and the newness and excitement of the amusement area with a "Walk of a Thousand Lights" that invited people to stroll near the large, crashing waves and to be entertained by Municipal Band concerts and numerous live and motion picture theaters.

Long Beach was nothing like his homeland Scotland and certainly more tolerable than San Bernardino. There were sunny skies and balmy breezes on most days. Light west winds blew across open fields of wheat and beans. Wide ranges of cattle and sheep dotted the several ranchos. Two rivers and streams teamed with fish running to the ocean. To the north were views of snow-capped mountains in the winter. What was not to love about Long Beach?

Because of his love of music, John must have enjoyed the Long Beach Marine Band concerts on Sunday afternoons given at the Pavilion, under the direction of D.W. Douglas. Some residents complained the band played too much classical music and not enough American marching music. Others loved listening to works of the masters, such as "Gloria" from *Twelfth Mass* by Mozart or the overture from Offenbach's *Orpheus*.

When he moved to Long Beach to care for his mother, John took the proceeds from the sale of his drugstore business and property in San Bernardino and opened a new drugstore at Pine Avenue near the post office. The business was adjacent to the W.W. Lowe general store. He became acquainted with the Lowes. William Lowe served as the city's first U.S.

A 1913 view of beach amusement area and municipal band shell. *Author's collection*.

postmaster. His wife, Belle, who suggested the name Long Beach for the city, helped establish the city's first school. She raised funds to pay for the first teacher, Grace Bush, a sixteen-year-old who taught students in a tent.

In Long Beach, John was just as dedicated to being involved with the church as he was to St. John's in San Bernardino. In 1905, he was elected to the vestry with several other prominent men in Long Beach, including L.H. Smith, and drew up a charter to change St. Luke's Protestant Episcopal Mission into a parish.

The mission had been established in 1897 by the Reverend Octavius Parker, who was replaced by the Reverend W.E. Jacobs. Jacobs had been assigned to Oceanside but then moved to San Pedro, riding horseback and alternating Sunday services between San Pedro and Long Beach. Jacobs laid the cornerstone for the first St. Luke's Church and remained pastor until 1901, when he was replaced by Reverend Charles T. Murphy, who stayed until 1906. Then the Reverend R.B. Gooden became pastor and grew the church membership to over four hundred. The new church was designed by architect Henry F. Starbuck and opened in 1910. Reverend Arnold George Henry Bode took over in 1912 and immediately began planning for a larger church to accommodate the growing ministry.

In 1905, Lamb sold his pharmacy to Harley Smith and then helped him obtain a city "druggist's license" to sell liquor. At that time, only licensed druggists could sell liquor, and the buyer had to have a letter from a physician.

Other things were happening in the city as well. The city's newly built pier burned in a fire caused by a faulty electric wire. In 1906, Hotel Bixby was constructed with reinforced concrete. Five stories of the central wing of the new $760,000 hotel collapsed, carrying nine men to their death in the tons of tangled wreckage. One hundred other men were injured. One of those severely injured was James Walsh, who languished for over a year before he died. His friends raised money to pay for the mortgage on his home so that his wife would not be faced with foreclosure. The contractor of the building blamed insecure footings on the sand and said they weakened the structure. The architects, however, said the disaster was caused because of the "premature removal of the support of the concrete work on the fifth floor, alleging that the cement had been given three, instead of six weeks to set." The collapse was written about in many construction and concrete publications.

That same year, newspapers featured headlines proclaiming, "Reign of Terror in Long Beach" due to a series of attacks on the homes of elected

Views of St. Luke's Episcopal Church. *Top: Library of Congress; Bottom: Author's collection.*

officials and public buildings by anonymous individuals. Mayor Rufus Eno claimed to have received a note threatening him with "disfigurement."

Someone doused Eno's house with oil so it could be set on fire. The home of the city marshal, J.J. Conklin, was dynamited while he and his family slept.

The voters of Long Beach and San Pedro were asked in 1905 to decide whether Long Beach could annex Terminal Island. The narrow strip of land between Long Beach and San Pedro was originally called Rattlesnake Island because of the number of snakes that came out after the rain overflowed the Los Angeles River. In 1891, it was renamed Terminal Island by the Los Angeles Terminal Railroad Company.

Because of the reports of terror and lawlessness in Long Beach, San Pedro voters almost defeated the annexation. When San Pedro lost, it contested the election results, alleging five ballots were illegally counted for annexation. Long Beach subsequently won the annexation of Terminal Island.

Mayor Eno resigned a year later after being arrested for taking a $350 bribe from an architect who wanted the contract to design the city's pleasure pier and sun parlor.

In 1905, John Lamb decided to sell his drugstore and join the Long Beach Savings & Trust Bank as a director and officer. He shared that distinction with several of the city's prominent Bixby men, George, Jotham and Llewellyn. His new position would free up his time to focus on the church, travel and his other interests.

John set about to secure funding so that St. Luke's Episcopal Church could have a building at Locust Avenue and Fifth Street. Later he would personally donate property located in the Bay View Heights area of the city to St. Luke's. His generosity toward the church went beyond Long Beach. From his own funds, he purchased a handsome Lenten stole and presented it to St. Peter's Church of San Pedro and the priest who had performed services at the Long Beach church.

John would also help raise funds to build a rectory at the Locust location in which the church minister and his wife would reside.

4

JOHN LAMB AND LOUIS HAZELWOOD SMITH

THE ONCE INSEPARABLE COUPLE

The men of the church vestry were John's dearest friends. He became close with them in his dedication to his church work, his love of music and in his personal real estate dealings, which he conducted with a local realtor, Louis Hazelwood Smith.

It was during his work at St. Luke's that John met Louis Hazelwood Smith. They became inseparable. They shared a common history of being from the British Isles and active members of the Episcopal Church. They worked together as trustees of the church and the vestry. They helped form the first chapter of the Long Beach Arcanum Council, a growing fraternal organization.

They both loved music. Sometimes John would play the piano to accompany L.H.'s sweet voice. Other times they would sing together, providing recitals at church services and social events. Their names were among those always listed at social events in Long Beach.

L.H. was an immensely attractive and popular real estate agent with

Passport photograph of Louis Hazelwood Smith. *U.S. National Archives and Records Administration.*

offices on the east oceanfront. He and his brothers were featured literally daily in the newspapers for their land transactions, their advertisements of properties for sale or their social and civic engagements.

John worked closely with L.H. in 1906, effecting the transfer of funds from relatives of the Crocker estate of San Francisco into the coffers of St. Luke's. Crocker Estate owned the Long Beach Development Company and a considerable amount of property in Long Beach, including the "library block" near Pacific Avenue and Ocean, which was used for the Carnegie Library.

John had been taken into the confidence of Alice King, a member of St. Luke's, who disclosed she had discovered the Crocker family of San Francisco owned two lots in Long Beach at Maine and First and were delinquent in their property taxes. King contacted the Crocker family and asked that the property be donated to St. Luke's.

With the help of John Lamb, the Crocker estate agreed to sell the property and share the proceeds of approximately $4,000 with St. Luke's.

L.H. handled the real estate transaction, and both he and John received headlines in the local newspapers for their efforts. They were both credited for putting St. Luke's in a strong financial position.

L.H. Smith seemed to be involved in every community and social organization in the city. He sold real estate from his office at 115 East Ocean and his home at 636 Chestnut Avenue.

John focused on church activities, supervising the Sunday school and the Brotherhood of St. Andrew for boys. He hosted numerous gatherings for the church and served as a delegate for church-related conventions. He entertained at piano and vocal recitals. The remainder of his time he traveled with his sister Marion, with whom she shared a house. His sister was a founding member of the Fifteen Friends group and hosted social gatherings frequently at their home.

Sample daily advertisement of Hazelwood-Smith Brothers Real Estate. *From the* Long Beach Press Telegram, *November 16, 1904.*

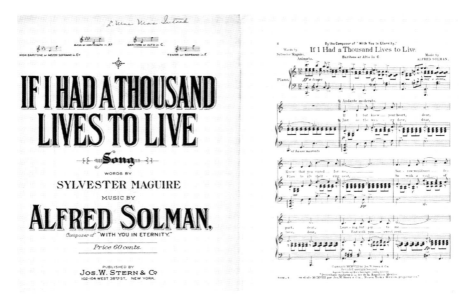

Sheet music of the song performed by L.H. Smith at Reverend Bode's anniversary party. *Library of Congress.*

John most likely noticed that L.H.'s behavior and attitude toward him changed dramatically once L.H. became an American citizen in May 1914. While newspaper articles frequently listed Lamb and Smith as attending the same social event, stories disappeared.

Their last social event together was a June 1 celebration for the wedding anniversary of St. Luke's rector and his wife. Both men sang solos.

John sang the Scottish "Annie Laurie," which was originally written by her sweetheart, William Douglas, and amended by Lady John Scott (1810–1900), who altered the second verse and composed the third. This song was a favorite with Scottish soldiers during the Crimean War.

L.H., on the other hand, who was seventeen years younger than Lamb, performed a romantic "If I Had a Thousand Lives" from the 1908 musical *The Heart Breakers.*

> *If I but knew your heart, dear,*
> *Knew that you cared for me,*
> *Sorrow would soon depart, dear,*
> *Leaving but joy to me.*

Loved one, whate'er you bid me,
I'd give my life to do,
And if this world were mine, dear,
I'd give it all to you!

CHORUS
If I had a thousand lives to live,
I'd live each one for you!
If I had a thousand hearts to give,
I'd give each one to you!
A thousand sorrows I would bear,
For one so fair so true,
If I had a thousand lives to live,
I'd live each one for you! live each one for you!

VERSE 2
Just as the weary dove, dear,
Flies to its sheltering nest,
So with a soul of love, dear,
I find with you sweet rest.
And as the twining ivy
Clings to the trembling vine,
So clings my heart to you, dear,
Yearning to call you mine!
*CHORUS**

Just two months later, a newspaper article reported a camping trip that L.H. organized on the Island of Santa Catalina for a fortnight with his brothers and another man.

Catalina is an island located twenty-six miles from Long Beach and was discovered by Juan Cabrillo in 1542. After it passed from Spanish control to Mexican control, it was owned privately as a resort island by Phineas Banning and his sons, who offered fishing excursions and other activities. It is twenty-seven miles long and one-quarter to seven miles wide. It has mountains and hills and a wild terrain perfect for camping.

---

* Source: Alfred Solman and Sylvester Maguire, "If I Had a Thousand Lives to Live" (1908), Historic Sheet Music Collection, 1630, https://digitalcommons.conncoll.edu/sheetmusic/1630. Readers can listen to an original recording of this song at: https://www.alexandria.ucsb.edu/lib/ark:/48907/f3x34w5q.

Early 1900s view of Catalina Island and camping tents. *Library of Congress.*

The *Long Beach Telegram and Daily Press* detailed the adventure:

> *After two most enjoyable weeks at Catalina Island Attorney George Hart, Percy, Leo, and Louis Hazelwood Smith returned to Long Beach Saturday evening, muchly tanned, and feeling "fine." They put in everyday fishing, boating, bathing, and playing tennis and brought home a record for having made the largest one-day catch of the season when they brought in 75 fish one afternoon. The catch included rock bass, white sea bass and a few yellowtails. They do not claim to have caught any particularly large fish, but state, in explanation, that no big fish are being caught at the island at all at the present time.*

John possibly understood why L.H.'s brothers were on the trip, but he most likely found it difficult to understand why Hart was invited and not he. For heaven's sake. Hart was a member of the Immanuel Baptist Church and supervised its Sunday school. L.H. was an Episcopalian like John.

On some level, John would have to admit that L.H. and Hart had some things in common. L.H. did the real estate transfer for Hart's home on Ocean Avenue and coordinated a lavish open house with music, flowers and art.

L.H. loved music, and Hart was an accomplished baritone singer.

L.H.'s real estate business depended on political connections. George Hart was politically ambitious and served as the city attorney for the small city of Watts north of Long Beach. Most significantly, George Hart was the son of the Police Court judge J.J. Hart. Senior Hart was also a former councilmember and city recorder and member of the Old Settlers Club, composed of the earliest white settlers of Long Beach. The club also included the politically ambitious newspaper reporter Eugene Irving Fisher.

One can just imagine how the thought of L.H.'s camping trip saddened John greatly. And how that sadness might have been the real reason he went out for a walk that fateful day in September. And how remembering L.H.'s trip with the Police Court judge's son George Hart might have been the reason Lamb named him in his suicide note.

5

LOUIS NAPOLEON WHEALTON

A TAMMANY HALL REJECT

J ohn Lamb was not the only one living in the oceanside town to notice how the horrible event that took place on May 24, 1913, seemed to signal a change in Long Beach.

On that day, Long Beach celebrated Empire Day, or Queen Victoria's birthday. The pilings near the entrance of the municipal pier collapsed under the weight of hundreds of women, children and elderly men waiting for the doors to open after the men and marched up Pine Avenue. Hundreds were injured. Thirty-three died.

Literally on the rubble of the collapsed pier wood, sand and bodies stood Louis Napoleon Whealton, New York attorney and political opportunist ready to take advantage of the tragedy. He encouraged families to sue the city over the collapse.

Louis N. Whealton was forty-one years old when he was elected mayor. He was married and had a son. The family lived at 1237 East First Street. He came to Long Beach in 1908 after spending some time in Mexico, where he had mining interests in the state of Sonora. He claimed he went to Mexico largely for the sake of his health.

Official portrait of Mayor Louis Napoleon Whealton. *Library of Congress.*

Whealton was born to Captain Joshua W. Whealton and Nancy C. Lewis in Accomack County, Virginia, on October 23, 1872, He grew up on Chincoteague Island, a remote place known for being inhabited by wild ponies. His father owned one hundred acres on the island, where he raised wild ducks, swans and geese.

Louis graduated from Johns Hopkins University and the University of Maryland. He had been a member of the legal bar for fifteen years and had practiced law since locating in Long Beach. He practiced law for seven years in New York City.

His World War I draft registration card indicates he was of "medium height, medium build, with brown eyes and brown hair."

Louis began seeking public office in New York. The *New York Tammany Times* wrote about Louis Whealton in 1900 that his nomination for Twenty-Third Assembly District was "without question one of the most popular selections that could have been made. Mr. Whealton is one of the most capable, energetic, and brainy young men....His election is a practical certainty."

Whealton lost by over three thousand votes.

He was an eloquent orator and prolific writer for local newspapers. Upon arrival in Long Beach, he joined numerous organizations to get his name before the public: the Royal Arch Masonic and Elks and Moose lodges, the City Club, the Merchants' and Manufacturers' Association, the chamber of commerce and the Coast Boulevard Association.

His Long Beach supporters claimed that when he ran for mayor in 1911 and 1913 he was not an "office seeker and that to serve as mayor of the city for two years means a sacrifice momentarily, that few men would be willing to bear."

Whealton repeatedly sought public office in Long Beach, using what was characterized by one prominent citizen as a "despicable campaign of trickery and deceit" that required he "belittle others to build himself up."

He was nicknamed "little Tammany" after the corrupt political group in New York. Over the years, he was criticized for changing political parties in order to launch a campaign. During his lifetime, he was a registered Democrat, a Progressive and a Republican.

Never one to miss an opportunity to try to woo women voters, Whealton arranged during his 1913 mayoral campaign for his campaign manager's daughter, Muriel Burdick, to "spontaneously" appear at a gathering and present him with flowers on behalf of the women of Long Beach, who wanted to thank him for "all he had done for suffrage." The press reported Whealton was so touched when Burdick spoke that "his eyes filled with tears."

Whealton tried reaching all available constituencies, including religious organizations. In 1911, he took up the cause of the local Mormons who were fighting against the city's prohibition of allowing their members to gather and speak on the public streets. He also made himself available to process the paperwork for the incorporation of the Unitarian Universalist Church and served on its board of trustees. His wife and son were members of the Protestant Episcopal Church, as was John Lamb.

Between campaigns, Whealton sued or threatened litigation against the city regarding rail lines, a privately constructed seawall and a city water department. He accused Councilman F.S. Craig, president of the public works commission, of graft and corruption, causing Craig to take out a full page in the *Long Beach Press* refuting Whealton's "libel."

In 1913, Long Beach still enjoyed a national reputation as a clean, sober city. Crimes were few and petty and were not reported. However, Whealton's campaign for mayor focused on convincing voters just how bad Long Beach really had become and how he could fix the city.

He wrote to the local press that he was:

> *not looking for glory, glory is not worth fighting for. I'd rather have chewing gum myself. Let us turn our faces to the future and to the city's urgent needs. Those are the things to be considered at the present time, not personalities. I contend that we want to put a stop to this thirty years' sleep and make Long Beach the city it ought to be and can be. I stand for aggressive, upbuilding work. I am opposed to this spineless, angel-worm policy of doing nothing and allowing no one else to do anything.*

Whealton took credit for things that happened in Long Beach before he even lived there, which resulted in one of his opponents remarking in the newspaper:

> *I don't know whether or not he takes the credit for the Los Angeles aqueduct. We ought to thank Whealton for the snow on Mount Baldy, for our bright sunshine and our excellent climate. We should give all credit to the man who put the pep in pepper and put the con in economy.*

The sentiment of concern about Whealton and what he might do to Long Beach was spelled out when former mayor, banker and councilmember C.J.

Walker announced that he would not serve on the city council if Whealton was elected mayor: "Strife and bickering would ensue. Life is too short for me to serve as a councilman under such circumstances."

Walker, a prominent banker, declared that it seemed strange to him how Long Beach got along before Whealton arrived and "how the City of New York manages to continue its existence without him."

Whealton won his election. Only 6,799 voted—less than 50 percent of those eligible. Whealton received 3,893 votes, his rivals Victor Humphreys received 2,806 and John Betts 100. C.J. Walker resigned after the election.

Charles Jabez Walker, councilman, mayor, realtor and founder of Farmers and Merchants Bank. *Greater Los Angeles and Southern California: Portraits, Robert Jones Burdette, 1910.*

6

WHEALTON CONDUCTS SECRET TRIALS AGAINST CITY STAFF

L ouis Whealton was an expert in stirring up trouble where none existed by suggesting Long Beach was more crime-ridden than it was.

Politics took on a vicious and personal tone when Whealton became mayor in late 1913. He threatened to fire the entire police and fire departments and the city librarian.

He began conducting secret trials of city staff, during which he was the prosecutor and the judge. He rounded up a councilman or two who supported him and used them to conduct these trials with him.

After the meetings, he would emerge and announce that he had "charges" that he could bring publicly against a city employee. However, if the employee resigned, they would be spared the public embarrassment of the residents knowing what ill they had done.

Whealton set about to engineer the forced resignation of the ever-popular city librarian Victoria Ellis. He appointed one of his major political contributors, Adelaide Tichenor, to head the library commission. Tichenor and Ellis had been friends and even traveled together extensively. Apparently, Tichenor was jealous of Ellis's popularity following the completion of the Carnegie Library and the visit to Long Beach by philanthropist Andrew Carnegie, during which he met with and acknowledged the librarian's work.

Tichenor teamed up with Whealton to set about to discredit the woman who assisted in the design and layout of the city Carnegie Library. Whealton used his newly formed library commission, headed by Tichenor, to demand from Ellis ridiculous information, such as:

Long Beach Carnegie Public Library, 1910. *Author's collection.*

What was the official name of the city library? Was it the Long Beach Carnegie Library? The Long Beach Public Library? The Carnegie Library of Long Beach?

The library commission also demanded that she compile an entire listing of thousands of library holdings and gave her only a few days to complete it by hand.

Ellis was a danger to a man like Whealton. She had compiled portfolios on over two hundred prominent men and women of the city. Each file was filled with clippings of news articles from across the United States—stories that were not published locally and were not known by the average Long Beach voter but could be read at the Long Beach Public Library.

Whealton once again claimed he had charges and told Ellis that if he released them to the public she would "lose all of her friends." Many good people of the town were outraged by his conduct, but they could not stop him.

Ellis confronted Whealton during a council meeting and challenged him to prove such charges, but the members of the council were not strong enough to overturn the inevitable. Victoria Ellis, who had served the city of Long Beach since 1903, resigned and left the area for the Orient, not to be heard from again for almost three years. When she returned to the

United States, she applied for the position of Orange County librarian but was turned down because of her difficulties in Long Beach.

Whealton had to turn his attention to battling some of the local newspapers when the *Long Beach Press* began publishing details of sordid dealings Whealton had with a private client, Florence Budd. Whealton was accused of conspiring with her to extort money from another woman.

The case involved an affair between Ida Morgan and Orris O. Budd. Morgan was the young widow of "Gold Dust" Morgan, a wealthy seventy-year-old racing and mining man who left her almost $250,000 and mines when he died. She met Morgan while working as a waitress at the Maryland Hotel in Pasadena. Budd was a foreman at one of her mines.

According to several news accounts, six men broke into the desert home of Mrs. Morgan and took a flashlight photograph of her in a compromising position with Mr. Budd. They then tried to "shake her down" for $50,000 and the $5,000 worth of diamonds she kept in a bag in her bedroom.

Apparently, the break-in was organized after Florence Budd, who suspected her husband was having an affair, contacted attorney Louis Whealton concerning the possibilities of suing Ida Morgan for "alienation of affections." With the help of Mrs. Budd's brother, E.P. Burroughs, R.E. Fisher, a private detective employed by Whealton, and four other men, a raid was planned on the Morgan home. The first attempt was called off when Mrs. Budd signaled that the pair was not at home.

The second attempt was successful. Mrs. Morgan recounted men broke into her home and "two detectives stood with revolvers leveled at her and Mr. Budd while they were taking the photograph for Mrs. Budd."

They bungled the photograph, and the flash made the figures unrecognizable, but the detectives threatened to testify that they had "sufficient evidence for an alienation suit" because of the adultery they had witnessed. During the raid, Mrs. Morgan alleged that her diamonds went missing.

Police arrested the six men who raided the home and Mr. Budd, who was accused of being involved in the plot to extort Mrs. Morgan.

Whealton denied doing anything illegal. But the repeated published accounts of the scandal forced him to be frequently absent from city hall in order to attend the Budd-Morgan trials. This slowed his plans to remove the chief of police and others in Long Beach.

When confronted by the press, Whealton said he had only instructed his investigator, Fisher, to serve papers on Mrs. Morgan for the lawsuit he was filing demanding $50,000 for the emotional injuries done to Mrs. Budd.

The charges against the six men were dismissed, but a trial was held on the issue of Mrs. Budd's claims.

Witnesses testified that on learning that Mrs. Budd knew of the affair, Mrs. Morgan had offered $20,000 to keep the affair quiet. They said Mrs. Budd responded she would have to discuss the matter with her attorney, Mr. Whealton. Whealton reportedly counseled her he could provide a list of Mrs. Morgan's heirs; he said she could tell them of the affair and "get what you can."

A grand jury was impaneled to investigate the allegations that Louis Whealton had participated in extortion. Facing the threat of recall from his position as mayor, Whealton begged the grand jury to "suppress certain letters and telegrams" he had sent. The judge refused. No indictment followed, but opposing counsel told the press that Louis Whealton was "a disgrace to the legal profession."

It was no secret Whealton had political ambitions beyond Long Beach. At some point, he realized he needed to make a name for himself nationally if he wanted to be elected to anything other than mayor of Long Beach.

Whealton took every opportunity to denounce the *Long Beach Press* newspaper for its coverage of the extortion trial and criticism of his actions as mayor. But he could not stop the momentum of some residents who were focused upon reforming Long Beach by changing the form of its local government.

When the freeholders of the city drew up a new charter to be voted on in a 1914 election, Whealton saw an opportunity to exploit the divisions

Cora Morgan was secretary to Board of Freeholders in 1914. *Long Beach Public Library*.

that were occurring among voters. Residents were divided over a proposed amendment to the city charter allowing the controlled sale of liquor to tourists visiting the Hotel Virginia and to residents in their own homes.

Whealton thought he had found the issue he could use to gain attention when he hired Samuel L. Browne, a private detective from Los Angeles, to secretly investigate his city's police department and expose corruption within.

Browne gathered evidence for Whealton and claimed that the current chief of police, A.B. Austin, and his detective captain, R.E. O'Rourke, had allowed gambling and wholesale "blind pigs" to flourish throughout the city and to sell liquor. The term *blind pig*

Talked of as Broadhead's Most Probable Successor

SAMUEL L. BROWNE

Samuel L. Browne was considered a candidate for Los Angeles police chief before coming to Long Beach. *From the* Los Angeles Herald, *March 31, 1909.*

was used for illegal places that sold alcohol and admitted patrons by viewing them through a small peephole in the door.

Browne upped his charges against the chief by accusing Austin of being publicly intoxicated and taking bribes. He accused O'Rourke with the same offenses but added "cruelty, brutality and inhumanity to prisoners."

Browne then issued twelve arrest warrants within two weeks of coming to Long Beach for operators of blind pigs, including several druggists. However, only one drugstore clerk was arrested. No one paid the fine of one hundred dollars. So, Whealton was unable to raise funds to pay for Sam Browne's fees.

Austin and O'Rourke denied the charges against them and demanded a public hearing and a reading of specific charges. Attorneys representing both Austin and O'Rourke complained that the eight charges against Austin and the six against O'Rourke lacked "definitiveness, specificness, and certainty."

Whealton thought these disclosures would be so scandalous to the voters that he would be a hero for uncovering them. However, he did not receive the support or gratitude he expected.

Many voters agreed that Whealton's actions were purely political and told newspaper reporters that he had been after the "scalp" of Chief Austin because he was part of the former charter party that Whealton defeated.

The *Los Angeles Times* criticized Whealton for making "spectacular promises to clean-up the town" that went unfulfilled. It went further to expose his political motivations by stating that his "spectacular denunciation of the police department" was made for a "double purpose," to boost the candidacy of Lynn W. Ballard for the council and to place Health Officer Ralph Taylor in the office of chief of police.

The *Press-Telegram* was very critical of Whealton. A 1914 article warned readers:

> *Whether one believes that Louis N. Whealton, the more or less distinguished mayor of this enterprising city, is a saint or a cynic; whether one believes he is a second Henry Clay, or just the ordinary kind of clay, with the Henry eliminated; whether one believes he is a crusader or a clown, a dub or a doctrinaire—whatever one believes, in short, regarding him one has to concede this: Our Whealtonian friend is one of the cutest little politicians that every pussy-footed down the macadamized highway.*

The *Los Angeles Times* followed up with accusations of C.C. Doran, that Whealton had approached him with a proposition to blackmail S.G. Barker, a candidate for city attorney, to get a plot of property valued at $3,000. Doran told the newspaper that Whealton said he would give him half of the $3,000.

Doran stated he refused to have anything to do with the affair and then accused Whealton of publicly defaming him because of his refusal to help blackmail Barker. Whealton had accused Doran, who was secretary of the Citizens Relief Committee, tasked to pay claims against the city for the Empire Day collapse of the pier, of using "vulgar and profane language to those who had suffered in the collapse." None of the accusations against Doran were substantiated.

Whealton continued his attack on Doran by accusing him of conspiring with his son, who worked in the District Attorney's Office to attempt to indict Whealton in relation to the Budd-Morgan case. Whealton also accused Doran of using former city librarian Victoria Ellis to go after him:

> *Miss Victoria Ellis twice resigned from the position of librarian. She resigned voluntarily and of her own accord. Previously I had asked her not*

to resign. I hoped when she did leave the office, she would go honored, loved and monumented for her ten years' work. But the black hand of politics reached forth for her. I knew that when they had used her to knock me, they would have no further use for her. I wanted her to leave office with the honor which she should, could and would have shown but the for contemptible politics of C.C. Doran.

The public fight between Doran and Whealton was vicious, as were many of Whealton's fights with others who crossed him.

Most of the public and the council staunchly defended the local police. This occurred partially because many in the city already knew that there was some gambling and liquor and looked the other way. Others knew the chief and officers being charged were from Long Beach and not from outside Long Beach like Browne. Even in this town, where temperance was held in high regard, it became more important to residents that they knew the people who were in their police department than which druggist illegally dispensed alcohol from his store.

After Whealton lashed out at the newspaper for his motives being questioned in removing the chief of police and replacing him with a Los Angeles detective, Sam Browne, the editors responded:

There may be people, in fact, there are many people, who think that the mayor is not quite ingenuous. But, after all, he is merely playing the game of politics. And if anyone thinks he is not playing it from the ground up, that individual is entitled to several more perfectly good guesses. No, fellow citizens, if you don't think there is a perfectly healthy game of politics going on right under your patrician noses, put a few facts in your meerschaums and smoke up.

Whealton did not relent. He took over the police department and installed Browne as chief of police. Browne was a colorful character who hired out to several cities to perform "detective work." In 1910, he was credited for extracting a confession from one of the McNamara brothers, who were accused of dynamiting the Los Angeles Times Building during a labor strike. His work earned him a $25,000 fee.

Browne's appointment as chief of police was controversial on so many levels. He was a resident of Los Angeles and would need to post a large bond guaranteeing his performance and return of any records in his possession when he left Long Beach. He also was vulgar and disrespectful to the members of the city police commission.

Eventually, several prominent members of the police department resigned under pressure of Whealton's "secret" investigations.

Certain citizens did not take kindly to the ouster of C.E. Snow, a police sergeant who was seriously injured during his heroic attempts at the time of the pier collapse in 1913.

Without the authority of the council, Whealton spent $500 on "secret services" to partially pay for Browne. He informed the council he also took out a loan from a local bank that the city "would have to repay."

Some of the press continued to publish articles concerning Whealton overdrawing the secret services fund and the lack of arrests of operators of blind pigs and gambling rooms.

The cries against Whealton's financial mismanagement increased. By early summer, many city department funds were already overdrawn.

Whealton met with the council and city officials to try to devise ways and means to tide the city over until September, when the new tax money was set to begin to come in. Until September, Whealton proposed that the banks tide the city over, when the city would be taken out of the "soak."

Whealton accumulated more debts by hiring Cora Morgan, a stenographer, who recorded minutes of his secret trials—work for which she was never paid and for which she had to sue the city.

He tried to deflect public criticism that he had spent more money on the secret service account than was ever before spent in twice the length of time by other mayors. The *Long Beach Press* questioned Whealton's claim to have made the city safer, citing that recent "hold-ups, nightly burglaries and a safe cracking" had taken place under his new police department because there were fewer police officers.

Even though the mayor did not have authority, Whealton instructed Browne to hire Christopher Cole for the police department. The City Civil Service Commission objected because Cole could not meet the physical requirements of a police officer. Browne was instructed by Whealton to appoint Cole as a secretary in the police department in order to get him on the inside and to be able to do Whealton's bidding.

Some of the newspapers invited Chief Austin to post columns to rebut allegations against him, calling Whealton "a liar." His biggest rebuke concerned Whealton's raid on the city treasury. Austin wrote:

> *Whealton and Browne and their political henchmen have some of the good people of Long Beach buffaloed into the honest belief that they have "cleaned up" Long Beach. I'll admit, judging by the condition of the secret service*

finances and the budget, that they have in one sense "cleaned" Long Beach;
but up to date their great flurry about catching blind pigs is mostly wind.

To counter the mounting criticism against him, Whealton took every opportunity to speak at public events. He garnered the support and admiration of the Woman's Christian Temperance Union, which unanimously passed a resolution praising him:

Resolved, in view of the fact that the Honorable Mr. Whealton, mayor of Long Beach, is trying to execute his official duty in a manly, courageous way, and should be commended by all temperance people.

While on one hand Whealton said he supported temperance and used city funds to investigate the illegal sale of liquor, he told the public he felt a proposed new charter was potentially "too dry" because it did not allow druggists to handle alcohol for any purpose.

Whealton failed to disclose that all the local druggists had requested this provision in the new charter, as they no longer wanted to dispense alcohol.

He purposely tried to dissuade those who favored loosening restrictions on alcohol from supporting the new charter. If passed by the voters on October 15, 1914, it would remove him as mayor the following July due to the fact that the form of government would change to a commission style. Five commissioners would be elected to govern public works, public safety, public affairs, public property, finance and accounting. One of them would be selected as mayor.

Whealton again turned his attacks on both the public works and the police departments. He accused the head of the board of public works of taking graft. Several members of the board resigned rather than face public humiliation with his accusations. He then battled with the city council, which would not confirm his appointments to replace board members who resigned.

However, once again he won accolades from some. The president of the chamber of commerce praised Whealton by telling the newspaper:

Mr. Whealton had stood by the orders of the Chamber of Commerce and executed them to the letter, with a manliness and fearlessness that could not be gainsaid.

Unfazed by the public criticism, Louis Whealton continued to spend even more city money. Many began clamoring for his recall as the city faced more and more problems and he took more funds. The *Long Beach Telegram* complained that the political bickering and recall petitions were causing damage to the image of the city:

> *Whether Mayor Whealton serves out his term is of small matter as compared with the question as to whether Long Beach forges ahead. She certainly cannot get ahead if perpetually hampered by strife and jarring and clashing and hubbub and rows and recalls. If the recall petition goes through and the recall election be made a fact, a crop of dragon's teeth will be sown in this particular area that will continue to develop armed men long after Mr. Whealton is forgotten.*

The pressure was increasing on Whealton. He needed to come up with a solution. Long Beach suffered considerable structural damage due to heavy rains and flooding in early 1914. Numerous lawsuits were being filed over the deaths and injuries caused by the Empire Day pier collapse.

Never to miss an opportunity to take advantage of chaos, Whealton saw a chance to use his appointed police chief to deflect criticism of his plundering the city treasury and his lack of management of city problems. He had a plan to not only bring in revenue but also raise this national profile—a plan that would end the life of John Amos Lamb.

7

WHEALTON FINDS SCHEME TO REPLACE DRAINED CITY SECRET SERVICES FUND

Whealton had a plan to not only bring in revenue to replace the funds he had spent but elevate his national profile as well. To do so, he first needed a way to distance himself from his close association with Reverend Benjamin Franklin Baker, the head of the First Unitarian Church of Long Beach.

Whealton served on the board of trustees that hired Baker in July 1913. Whealton immediately placed Baker in a prominent position on his mayoral campaign, letting him author many of the publications used to promote "Whealton for Mayor." Baker also served as his surrogate, representing him during the city Fusion Party meetings to gather support for his candidacy.

On October 10, 1913, months before Whealton's election, the Reverend Baker was arrested as a "lewd vagrant."

The details of the Baker scandal ran in most California newspapers, followed by the story that the church board of trustees, headed by Whealton, gave Baker a six-month leave of absence after his arrest. Whealton needed to make certain the Baker connection went no further.

Interestingly, around the same time, the newspapers made little of the fact that George H. Bixby, son of Jotham Bixby—the "father of Long Beach"—was named in a "white slavery case" in which he was accused of having procured young women for other men and contributing to the delinquency of a minor.

Both Bixby and John Lamb were elected officers of the same Long Beach Savings Bank and Trust Company, but the newspaper and public reaction to their behavior would be quite different.

Bixby admitted to frequenting the Jonquil apartments, at 807 Hill Street in Los Angeles, known as "a place of certain immoral standing." The location was often referred to as "the roadhouse resort in the village of Vernon, on the rim of Los Angeles where it is alleged, lent itself to the debaucher of girls of minor age."

Bixby testified that he visited the Jonquil "only as a Samaritan who spent thousands to save young girls."

More than fifty prominent men of Long Beach testified to Bixby's moral character. Many argued that Bixby, a man of considerable wealth, was being blackmailed by a group of men and women who were actually involved in the procurement of women.

Several young women testified against Bixby and claimed that he was referred to by the young women who were made available at the Jonquil as "The Black Pearl," or "Mr. King." They also claimed he gave each of "his girls" a gold cross, which they wore around their necks during the court trial.

The judge ruled that the women were not allowed to testify about their relations with Bixby, which seriously weakened the case against Bixby. However, one of the young women who had filed a lawsuit against Bixby was

Home of early settler Jotham Bixby, father of George Bixby, located on bluff overlooking the Pacific Ocean. *Author's collection.*

RED LIGHTS IN THE SPOTLIGHT.

Grand Jury Starts General Vice Inquiry.

Bench Warrant's Issued for Millionaire Bixby.

He Doesn't Appear; Police Can't Find Him.

A bench warrant issued for George H. Bixby, the Long Beach millionaire, subpoenaed as a witness against Josie Rosenberg, alleged procuress, because the financier was absent at the preliminary examination yesterday afternoon, and the taking of testimony of several women of the underworld were the principal features of yesterday's investigation of supposed

George Bixby resisted a subpoena for trial on "white slavery." *From the* Los Angeles Times, *April 24, 1913.*

allowed to testify that the suit was being brought because he had assaulted her. When asked to explain, she said that Bixby had committed a "revolting act" against her.

His attorneys turned the attention to the claimed extortion of Bixby and away from his active participation with the young women—many underage.

Bixby was found not guilty. There was no local editorial outcry like there would be later when Herbert Lowe and Charles Espey were also found not guilty of being "social vagrants."

In contrast to what would be published on the men arrested in Long Beach the following year, the *Los Angeles Times* editor wrote before the Bixby verdict:

> *His townspeople and hundreds of friends have faith in Bixby, and declare no scandal will attach to his name when the situation clears and the facts come out.*

Sacramento Bee editor and publisher C.K. McClatchy lashed out when Sacramento was accused by some local residents as being "immoral." He wrote:

> *This page has yet to hear in this city of Jonquil Clubs that flourish as the green bay tree in Loses, or of homosexual organization such as made the name of Long Beach a by-word and a reproach.*

There is absolutely no more immorality in Sacramento per 1,000 of population or inch by inch, than there is among the aureoled cities of Southern California.

The bepuffed Los Angeles is absolutely honeycombed with assignation houses, and its thoroughfares fairly alive with persuading street-walkers.

Yet you do not find any one in Los Angeles not even the ministers, standing at the gateway like the Judean lepers, warning visitors away and croaking out, "Unclean! Unclean!"

Mayoral candidate Louis Whealton never uttered a single word about the Bixby trial or the plight of the young women who were trafficked for the pleasure of wealthy men. But he would be very vocal about his campaign against "men who made advances to other men."

8

THE STATE OF SODOMY

Whealton was planning on running for the state assembly, so he went out on the speaking circuit throughout Southern California on behalf of Frank Roberts, Republican candidate for U.S. Congress. In return, he was introduced to crowds of voters as the "Mayor of Long Beach, an ardent worker for temperance and morality."

Not coincidentally, Roberts was the editor and publisher of the *Long Beach Daily Telegram*, which gave Whealton frequent, favorable coverage.

Between speeches and glad-handing, Whealton continued his changes in the police department and managed to get C.C. Cole promoted from police secretary to sergeant to acting chief of police. Cole was more than pleased to do Whealton's bidding and agreed to secretly bring to Long Beach two special officers who had been employed by the Los Angeles Police and lived in the cities of Venice and Los Angeles.

The special officers, W.H. Warren and B.C. Brown, had worked under Chief Sebastian of Los Angeles. Neither had official police training, and they worked for cash bounties, being paid ten dollars for each man they arrested. They boasted they had "special ways" of knowing which men to go after and how to get evidence from these "lewd vagrants."

They originally came to Los Angeles from Chicago, where Brown was employed in the William J. Burns Detective Agency. Warren was connected at one time with the *Sacramento Bee* and the *Star* newspapers, working in their business offices. Both Warren and Brown worked on salary in Los Angeles. According to a report from Eugene Fisher, the special officers were put on a

Christopher C. Cole was appointed chief of police in 1913. *Long Beach Police Officers Pictorial, 1928.*

"bounty" in Long Beach because "the Police Commission would not allow a salary believing there was nothing like 'social vagrancy' existing here."

Warren was described in court proceedings as a "good-looking man with rugged looks." Brown was described as "having the facial appearance of a woman, with slicked back hair and lightly pink-tinted fingernails."

Even though they were neither from Long Beach nor familiar with the town, they were given Long Beach police stars to wear. They were directed by Whealton and Chief Cole to do whatever they had done in Los Angeles "to get evidence against a coterie of men whose unnatural tendencies caused them to make advances to other men." Whealton and Cole thought that Warren and Brown could attract various sorts of other men. And they did.

This work was all a matter of a joke to "Billy" Warren, who boasted he could make a good living—fifty, seventy-five, even one hundred dollars and sometimes more.

The men planned on to go to city after city all over the country selling their services. They were turned down in the city of Venice, California, because it was rumored that one of the members of the police commission himself was "a member of the queers."

Whealton hid his plan from most of the city council and from the voters, who still clamored for arrests of owners of liquor and gambling places.

Neither Whealton nor Police Chief Cole asked about how these special officers collared men or how it was they witnessed their behavior. They did not care about the ways Warren and Brown found to ensnare these men in the public comfort station and haul them away to the local police judge, J.J. Hart. Hart would charge the men, fine them up to $500 and send them home if they pleaded guilty. The men who could not afford the fines were sent to jail for six months.

Eugene Fisher remarked in his notes to C.K. McClatchy:

One thing is noticeable and that is that there was not a laborer in the entire list and men of affairs who really are busy are conspicuous by absence from the lists of social vagrancy. It apparently attracts the indolent, the men who have money and lots of idle time and in this respect, California the meccas of tourists may possibly have a larger percent of "queers" than some of the other large cities.

When entrapping men at the public comfort station was not enough, Warren and Brown targeted a popular local florist in his own home.

The issue of men making "advances to other men" was not a frequent topic of the Long Beach newspapers. In fact, newspapers in other states, such as Kansas, published story after story about the "wave of sensuality— one might say sodomy" that had "spread through the length and breadth of this land."

Long Beach newspapers briefly mentioned the "vice scandals" that took place in 1912 at the Portland, Oregon YMCA. They never mentioned the other story that was featured in the Northwest about a young woman, Nell Pickerel, who lived their life dressed as a man and referred to themselves as "Harry Allen." Allen was the subject of many newspapers in Seattle and elsewhere when it was disclosed that they "worked as a longshoreman, straddled bronchos, rode a men's bicycle, engaged in prizefighting and wooed many ladies."

In 1912, the Portland police arrested a nineteen-year-old on a minor charge who while in custody provided details about the YMCA being used by men as a gathering place to seduce younger men.

Several prominent Portland men were arrested and convicted on sodomy charges. Sodomy was characterized in law as the "infamous crime against nature either with a man or a beast." In order to arrest someone and charge with sodomy, there needed to be an eyewitness to the act. Also, sodomy was anal sex and did not include oral sex or other sexual behavior between men.

In California, a broader law of "lewd vagrancy" was used to arrest a man engaging in such activities. These men were referred to as "social vagrants. "

A citizen committee investigated and claimed that the Portland YMCA was in no way connected with the activities. They had nothing to do with the men who rented rooms. Nevertheless, the story sparked sensational stories outside of Long Beach alleging that those kinds of activities were a widespread danger across the country and needed to be stopped.

The Long Beach newspapers did briefly cover the arrest of Unitarian minister Franklin Baker in 1913. Born Benjamin Franklin Baker in 1876, he was profiled in newspapers as a "minister, scion of a prominent family in Connor, Kansas and baseball athlete." In fact, Franklin and his two brothers were raised by their mother, who divorced the boys' father on the basis of "abandonment."

Franklin attended university in Lawrence, Kansas. As a member of the drama club, he appeared in a number of performances and was billed as "an impersonator." Newspaper critics noted that Baker "as usual over-did the part" whenever he appeared in a play.

Baker also attended the Chicago Theological Seminary and then did special studies at Cambridge University, England, and Heidelberg, Germany. He was ordained in the Norfolk, Nebraska Congregational Church in March 1902.

He served as minister in Colorado Springs, Colorado; Norfolk, Nebraska; Yakima, Washington; and Stockton, Eureka and Sacramento, California.

Baker increased the membership in Sacramento from forty to seventy-eight. While in Sacramento, he edited a religion column in the *Sacramento Bee*. His sermons were perhaps the most outrageous of any minister, which brought him national notoriety. He applied for a leave of absence in 1913 due to his wife's ill health. He resigned on April 30.

He was often confused in the press with another Sacramento minister named Franklin Baker, who served as chaplain for the state legislature. The other Baker frequently received criticism for the sermons delivered by the other man.

Several sermons garnered him the most notice: "Why Unitarians Believe in Dancing, Card Playing, Theaters and Going to the Circus," "The Good in Sunday Baseball and Casey at the Bat" and "Why Divorce Is Preferable to Unhappy Marriages and Why I Marry Divorcees."

Baker was rather unpopular with the other ministers of the town because they did not agree with his style of preaching. Besides, he would have nothing to do with them socially.

Baker suddenly left his ministry in Sacramento in January and announced he was traveling to Alaska in search of gold. He and his wife, Effie, moved in April 1913 and came to Long Beach to incorporate the First Unitarian Church and clubhouse at Third Street and Cedar Avenue.

The Reverend Franklin Baker preached the first sermon in Long Beach in April 1913. The next week, the church was officially organized in the law offices of Louis N. Whealton, candidate for mayor. Sixty-three people joined with twenty-eight charter members.

In Long Beach, Baker became wildly popular with the members of his church—many of whom were powerful people in the city, such as Whealton.

Baker announced in a September meeting that he had secured $5,500 from the American Unitarian Association for a new building. He then launched into his talk, "Why a Unitarian Church in Long Beach." He used "Ye shall know the truth, and the truth shall make you free" as a text:

> *Because there is no other church more broad in its conception of life, humanity, the universe and God. Because the Unitarian Church is builded [sic] upon the recognition of divine intelligence both in man and the world about him. Because this church recognizes the reason of every individual as the ultimate authority in all matters religious, the intellect as superior to the authority of any book or tradition.*
>
> *The religion of the Unitarian Church is free, not creed bound; scientific, not dogmatic; spiritual, not traditional; universal, not sectarian. It stands for the realization of the highest moral and humanitarian ideals of the world's noblest teachers and the cultivation and dissemination of the spiritual qualities of reverence, peace and love as exemplified in the life of Jesus of Nazareth.*
>
> *The membership roll of the Unitarian Church is open to the signature of every man or woman interested in trying to make this life a happier one in which to live. It asks no theological questions of its adherents, save "love to God and man." Its only disciplinary requirement is that each one in its fellowship shall do his own thinking. In matters of religion, the Unitarian Church offers no panacea for the world ills save love; has no inducements to offer for soul salvation save, character.*
>
> *Long Beach is destined to be a large city, hence many more people of liberal religious ideas will be making this city their home. There are at least twenty thousand more members in Long Beach. It is for the non-churched that the Unitarian church exists.*
>
> *The Unitarian idea of amusements is based upon the concept of "to the pure all thing are pure." Hence it believes in the cultivation of those harmless amusements, which the conservative church condemns.*
>
> *Its church buildings are constructed with the idea of the church being a spiritual social center for the family and its friends.*

Baker formed the "women's alliance of liberal women, an auxiliary of the Unitarian Church," reported the *Long Beach Telegram and Long Beach Daily News* in December 1913.

Because all the other churches in Long Beach held services on Sunday evenings, the city concert band canceled Sunday evening concerts. Baker immediately challenged the lack of "separation of church and state" and changed the Unitarian Sunday services to begin at eleven o'clock in the morning. He called on the band to reinstate the evening concerts since "that is what the taxpayers paid them to do."

He became a member of the Long Beach Elks Lodge. He socialized at the Signal Hill Tennis Club with the Smith brothers, Leo and L.H. He filled in for attorney Louis Whealton as the featured speaker at programs discussing patriotism on Flag Day.

Baker joined Whealton's campaign for mayor and became his surrogate speaker until the afternoon of October 9, 1913, when two Los Angeles detectives arrested him in Santa Monica.

In addition to incorporating a church in Long Beach, Franklin Baker claimed to be organizing a congregation in Santa Monica, north of Long Beach, which is also in Los Angeles County. It was in Santa Monica where two plainclothes detectives arrested him in broad daylight and charged him with trying to make "advances toward men."

The arrest took place on a crowded street outside a public auction where Baker said he was browsing. In one report, it was alleged that Baker tried to "feel up" a police detective. Two detectives, listed as Burgess and Sayre, told Baker that they had been "shadowing" him for ten days after receiving a complaint by an unnamed man to issue a warrant for his arrest. The man suggested that they keep "a close eye on his actions."

Baker was taken to the Los Angeles jail. There he called one of his Long Beach congregants, Juvenile Court judge Fred H. Taft. Taft arrived at the jail and personally vouched for Baker's innocence. Baker cried as he proclaimed that his arrest was "nothing but an attempt to blackmail and ruin his character."

On returning to Long Beach, Baker contacted another close friend, Roland Swaffield, to serve as his attorney for the jury trial he requested, so he could prove his innocence.

The story of Baker's arrest appeared in many newspapers, including the *Sacramento Bee*, whose editor, C.K. McClatchy had taken a special interest.

The *Sacramento Bee* featured these front-page headlines: "Rev. Franklin Arrested as 'Vag' Well Known Here." "Reverend Franklin Baker, Formerly of This City, Disgraced in South."

Eugene Irving Fisher contacted his former employer, C.K. McClatchy, while working as a Long Beach reporter and attending law school. He offered to provide him with details on Baker, who left Sacramento hurriedly just four months prior. McClatchy was convinced that Baker was part of a larger group of "degenerates" and wanted proof of his conduct in Long Beach.

Eugene Fisher, who had returned to Long Beach from Sacramento, not only provided McClatchy details on Baker but later also disclosed the inside details of Whealton's "secret plan" to entrap homosexual men.

According to Fisher, Baker broke down and told acting chief of police Sam Browne that he was a "fruiter."

Interestingly, McClatchy was at first reluctant to publish the information sent by Fisher:

> *I have read over your statement from Long Beach and Los Angeles concerning the "social vagrancy" question with a great deal of interest, mingled with disgust. I want you to keep right on with the matter and get me everything you possibly can.*
>
> *Of course, your dope so far sent could not be used as written; and when I say that I have no reference particularly to the words here and there which certainly could not be used in a paper—but I have reference to the general tenor of it. Of course, I understand that it was not written as it reads for publication; but that under my instructions you got hold of everything you possible could and turned in all the details.*
>
> *You say in your letter that you think the authorities at Los Angeles are trying to protect the more prominent guilty. Can you get more dope upon this subject, focusing to the front of the big ones?*
>
> *I do not want to publish anything for some time unless there is fear of a Los Angeles paper jumping in. If that should ever occur or you see symptoms of it, tip me by telegraph.*
>
> *I thought after receiving your next assortment of names, etc., I would have a general strong article made upon the subject and then wait a few days for the writing up of a second article. I thought also that if there were any danger you would not be able to clinch things down there, I could send someone down from here for two or three days to piece up the ragged edges. I know it is pretty hard job for you to do, while at the same time doing your work on the Press.*

McClatchy filled the remainder of his letter to Fisher with specific questions of the scandals in Los Angeles and Long Beach.

Fisher needed an "insider" who could give him more details about the "society of queers" that was rumored to operate in Long Beach and Los Angeles. He found L.I. Rollins, who was arrested during a large snare of "social vagrants" in Los Angeles. Rollins was more than willing to talk. Fisher interviewed him and sent frequent dispatches to McClatchy.

Fisher's reports were titillating and salacious. He explained to McClatchy:

> *You are mistaken, however, as to the offense of which they are guilty. The majority of these cases, in fact all that I have mentioned as having pled guilty in Long Beach and been given jail sentences or fines, are known to the officers as "fruiters" and their offense is nothing more nor less that [sic] "cock sucking."*

If Rollins were to be believed, there were several "secret societies" at which men would gather and array themselves in:

> *kimonos, loosely hung from the shoulders, put on silk underclothing, long silk stockings, French heeled slippers, rouge their faces and then proceed to the revels. Some of the men even wore women's wigs. The members of these societies were made up for the stages as if they were performing.*

McClatchy responded to Fisher's details that "Dr. Hirschfeld might not be far astray concerning conditions in the United States." Dr. Magnus Hirschfeld was a proponent of homosexuality and wrote about the growing numbers in Germany and the United States.

Within three days of Franklin Baker's arrest, Louis Whealton called together the board of trustees of the Unitarian Church and proposed granting Baker a "six-month vacation," during which he could plan his defense. Baker was replaced by Reverend Francis Watry, and services were moved to the Ebell Clubhouse.

Whealton drafted a resolution that was unanimously adopted by the trustees:

> *Expressing its unqualified faith in his innocence and belief in his integrity and character as a pastor and man and pledging him our hearty and united effort in restoring to him the good reputation he has always enjoyed in this and all other communities in which he has lived.*

Baker in turn issued a written denial of the charges:

> *Affirming my innocence before God and Man and recognizing the fact that my every energy must be devoted, from now until my case is heard*

by a jury of my peers, to the work of preparing for this crisis, I request the board of trustees of the First Unitarian Church of Long Beach to give me a vacation of sixty days in order that I may be unhampered in the preparation of my defense, and that the church may not suffer in the meantime through my misfortune.

Baker's trial was postponed and rescheduled several times and finally dismissed. Baker disappeared from Long Beach, never to be heard from again.

The dismissal of Baker's trial enraged C.K. McClatchy in Sacramento. He contended that it was "money and influence" that allowed Baker, a "confessed degenerate," to escape punishment. He also blamed the newspapers in Southern California, which "gave little space to the Baker case because the public took little interest in it."

McClatchy alleged that Samuel L. Browne, whom he described as having a "national, if not international reputation as a public and private investigator of crimes and criminals," gave him a written statement after interviewing Baker on October 11:

Baker confessed to me that he is a degenerate, including his methods of solicitation. I know he is such and you may say that I said so. I know why his case was dismissed. Influence has brought to bear, and yet again influence.

McClatchy was determined that degeneracy, which he called "this monstrous evil that was eating into the people of Germany," was widespread. When a German expert on sexual behavior also published his findings that there were over "500,000 homosexuals in the United States," McClatchy was more than willing to do what he could to root out the "evil that was among us and spreading."

Fisher kept reminding McClatchy:

There is no law under which this crime against nature is punishable directly, hence they are arrested and prosecuted as "social vagrants" and lewd and dissolute persons.

This enraged McClatchy, who went on a campaign to convince his friends in the California legislature to make oral copulation between men a felony.

9

LONG BEACH LAUNCHES PUBLIC COMFORT STATION

M any public health officials campaigned for "public comfort stations" in cities as a way to afford people an opportunity to "eliminate from the body waste products that become poisonous by retention." People had to rely on toilets in saloons, and since Long Beach outlawed saloons, it needed to provide public comfort stations in other locations. Cities, such as Long Beach, were slow to construct and operate public comfort stations because they were an expense taken out of public works budgets.

In nearby San Pedro, the problems created by comfort stations were hotly debated:

> The comfort station has been a disgrace to San Pedro for years. Its location invites lots of drunken roughnecks and janitors have had a hard time keeping it in usable condition. E.D. Seward, custodian of the city hall, has recommended that it be closed entirely. The chamber of commerce recently asked the city council to provide funds to build a new comfort station under the steps in the city hall but instead $600 was recommended by the committee to fix up the old one. With a great number of strangers in San Pedro every day the need of a comfort station has been most apparent. There is not hotel in San Pedro and no public place where ladies can go without being put to the embarrassment of asking private accommodations from business houses and other.

In 1912, Long Beach offered two public "comfort stations" where men and women could use toilets and freshen up. One was in the basement of the Carnegie Library. The other was in the outer lower area of the auditorium.

The Long Beach Chamber of Commerce and other businessmen petitioned the city to construct a new public comfort station to accommodate the tourists and residents who came to the downtown area near the Walk of a Thousand Lights, that area along the Long Beach Bathhouse that included shops, amusements and theaters, offering moving pictures and vaudeville.

Throughout the United States, specifications for "public comfort stations" had been developed:

> *Partitions Between Fixtures. Adjoining water-closets shall be separated by partitions. Every individual urinal shall be provided with a partition at each end and at the back to give privacy. Where individual urinals are arranged in batteries a partition shall be placed at each end and at the back of the battery. A space of 6 to 12 inches is required between the floor end the bottom of the partition. The top of the partition shall be from 5½ to 6 feet above the floor. For water-closet compartments used by women, doors of the same height as required for partitions shall be installed. Doors from 3 to 4 feet high, with the bottom from 8 to 10 inches above the floor, shall be provided for men. Toilet compartment doors shall be made of wood or metal. All partitions shall be of material and finish as prescribed for walls and ceilings.*
>
> *Walls, Ceilings, Partitions. The walls, ceilings and partitions shall be completely covered with smooth cement of gypsum plaster, glazed brick, or title, galvanized, painted, or enameled metal, or other smooth non-absorbent material. Wood may be used if well covered with two coats of body paint and one coat of enamel paint or spar varnish. But wood shall not be used for separating walls or partitions between toilet rooms, nor for partitions which separate a toilet room from any room used by the opposite sex. All such partitions shall be practically soundproof.*

In August 1910, the *Long Beach Press* previewed the design of the comfort station by W.H. Austin:

> *Reproduced Illustration from the Design of Architect W.H. Austin*
> *It is a matter of common comment that no public improvement is more urgently needed by the city than the proposed new Public Comfort Station.*

The above illustration is a reproduction of the design drawn by Architect W. H. Austin. The proposed building, if constructed, will make one of the city's sightly and attractive features. The building of this station will also constitute an advertising asset for the city. As it is deemed it is believed that the revenue desirable from rental space will meet the cost of maintenance. The building is planned to be of reinforced concrete, 20x152 feet in size, to be located at the foot of Pine avenue in and on the bluff south of the Salt Lake railway depot. It provides for a ladies rest and dressing room, which will be of marble finish, with mirrors, etc. The interior of both departments will have white marble finish. The plan also provides for a janitor's or caretaker's room. There's a provision also for rental space for newsstands, boot-black stands, etc. The plan

PROPOSED PUBLIC COMFORT STATION, BEAUTIFUL DESIGN

INTERIOR FINISH IS PLANNED TO BE IN WHITE MARBLE

REPRODUCED ILLUSTRATION FROM THE DESIGN OF ARCHITECT W. H. AUSTIN.

It is a matter of common comment that no public improvement is more urgently needed by the city than the proposed new Public Comfort Station. The above illustration is a reproduction of the design drawn by Architect W. H. Austin. The proposed building, if constructed, will make one of the city's sightly and attractive features. The building of this station will also constitute an advertising asset for the city. As it is deemed it is believed that the revenue desirable from rental space will meet the cost of maintainance. The building is planned to be of reinforced concrete, 20x152 feet in size, to be located at the foot of Pine avenue in and on the bluff south of the Salt Lake railway depot. It provides for a ladies' rest and dressing room, which will be of marble finish, with mirrors, etc. The interior of both departments will have white marble finish. The plan also provides for a janitor's or caretaker's room. There is a provision also for rental space for news stands, boot-black stands, etc. The plan contemplates that every feature and fixture of the proposed structure shall be strictly of the best material and of the most modern designs. The sanitary arrangement is thorough. Exhaust ventilators are planned to operate through the column in the center. Architect Austin states that the total cost of construction will not exceed $15,000 and will likely come under that figure.

Drawing of proposed public comfort station designed by W.H. Austin. *From the* Long Beach Press, *August 11, 1910.*

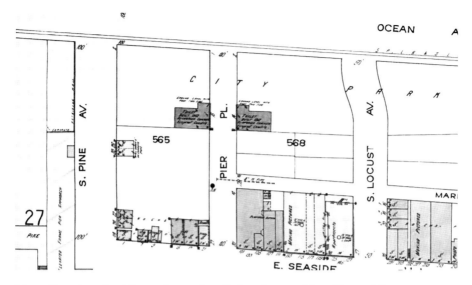

Map of location of public comfort station. *Sanborn Insurance Maps, Library of Congress.*

contemplates that every feature and fixture of the proposed structure shall be strictly of the best material and of the most modern designs. The sanitary arrangement is thorough. Exhaust ventilators are planned to operate through the column in the center. Architect Austin states that the total cost of construction will not exceed $15,000 and will likely come under that figure.

Long Beach added the third public comfort station in 1912 on Pier Place located south of the San Pedro, Los Angeles and Salt Lake City Railroad and Ocean Avenue at the foot of Locust. Nearby was the Municipal Auditorium, which was partly over water. The "double deck Pleasure Pier" jutted out over the ocean one thousand feet to the sun parlor and vendor booths at the end of the structure. Steps away were a bandstand and pergola at which the Municipal Band played most days.

The local newspaper bragged:

[The structure was a] *credit to Long Beach and one of finest in the country. It is up to date, in every respect, sanitary, well ventilated, well-lit, and clean. The twin structures, one for men and one for women, are built on either side of the way, leading from Ocean Ave to the beach, and are ideally located, for buildings of this sort.*

It cost the city $4,100 for the reinforced concrete comfort station. The Pacific Electric Railroad, the Salt Lake Railroad and the Long Beach Bath House company were expected to contribute to the cost of building the structure. The city was to pay for maintenance and budgeted a janitor to clean the male side and a janitress to assist the women.

The wooden partitions between urinals would play a major factor in the entrapment of men by the special officers hired by Whealton.

10

LAMB'S FATEFUL STROLL ALONG THE WALK OF A THOUSAND LIGHTS

J ohn Lamb was known for his early-morning habit of reading the *Los Angeles Times* while he took tea. The newspaper that day was filled with headlines and stories about the war raging in Europe. As usual, there was no mention of Long Beach.

On page 6 of section II of the newspaper, the regular column "Laura Jean Libbey Talks Heart Topics" might have been something Lamb found relevant to his situation with L.H. Smith.

> *O we fell out, I know not why,*
> *And kiss'd again with tears,*
> *And blessings on the falling out.*
> *That all the more endears.*
> *The old beau is steady, having sown his wild oats, if he had any....*
> *Such men form habits which grip them with so firm a hold that they seldom*
> *or never are enabled to shake themselves free from....*
> *Time passes over his head and he finds that he craves a still younger love*
> *each year....*

John Lamb set out for a walk. He most likely had not been in the newest public comfort station before that Tuesday, September 22, 1914. He lived just several blocks from the beach strand in a comfortable bungalow on Broadway. Public comfort stations were meant for the visitor who had no other access to toilets.

To reach the comfort station, Lamb would have to walk south from Broadway. He would then be near the Pike Walk of a Thousand Lights, named for Thomas Edison's incandescent white and purple lights strung across the boardwalk area, creating a carnival-like atmosphere at night. He could also take a trolley from Broadway.

That area included the Majestic Dance Hall and the Long Beach Bathhouse and Plunge with its five hundred dressing rooms. Bathers could swim inside in salt water piped from the ocean. There was a bowling alley next door, the largest on the West Coast area, and moving picture theaters and live vaudeville on both sides of the walk. The designers made the area appear as if it were a miniature Coney Island with games, an "airship ride," a Loof carousel and other attractions.

Walk of a Thousand Lights, named for the incandescent bulbs along the walkway. *Library of Congress*.

A 1914 photograph of the roller coaster and businesses along the Walk of a Thousand lights. *Author's collection*.

It is not known why John Lamb decided to take a walk on that particular day along the strand, which faced the ocean, near the auditorium, bathhouse and pier.

Maybe it was his position with Long Beach Savings Bank & Trust that called on him to personally view the properties along the strand.

Residents were becoming more concerned that the beach meandering alongside the Walk of a Thousand Lights and the Pike area would be developed with more and more amusements and cluttered with concessions. The city did not own the beach, and a citizen committee urged a consortium of banks to assess the property and determine the cost for it to be acquired through a vote from the Long Beach Bathhouse and Amusement Company.

John Lamb and other bankers assessed the land south of Ocean Avenue to the water's edge to be worth $736,000. If voters approved bonds, the property would be purchased by the city, and the deed would dedicate the beach exclusively as public playgrounds, prohibiting obstructions of any sort south of Seaside Walk for all time, perpetuating its natural beauty. All buildings and concessions south of the walk would be removed, leaving a beautiful open beach for time indefinite, dedicated exclusively for bathing,

Front view of Long Beach Bathhouse with fully dressed sunbathers. *Author's collection.*

recreation and playground purposes and to the benefit of residents, visitors and posterity.

The vote on the bonds would be held later that month, so John could justify a personal visit to the property in question.

It was high tide when John arrived for his walk. His and Marion's home at 3237 Broadway was not terribly far from the ocean. The waves were unusually high, breaking and battering and pounding, a sight made more glorious by the sunny skies.

Long Beach had been hit by tremendous storms earlier in January, which closed the pier and shops and flooded parts of the city. It had taken some time for the repairs, but the pier and boardwalk were again open.

No doubt John, like other residents, came here for many occasions. In April 1908, fifty thousand residents gathered as the U.S. Navy's Great White Fleet steamed across the Pacific and anchored off the coast of Long Beach. President Theodore Roosevelt ordered the naval ships painted white and sent them around the world to show off the United States' naval power. The event featured many festivities. including the citizens hosting the sailors and officers to a barbecue of the finest beef donated by Jotham Bixby from his nearby Rancho Los Cerritos. Lamb and the vestry hosted California governor James Gillett at St. Luke's on Sunday for both morning and evening services.

John loved to travel, so the newly introduced aviation along the beach must have been interesting to him. Residents who came to the beach could watch planes being flown low, sometimes landing on the sand and then taking off into the air. Occasionally, balloonists would soar over the Pine Avenue Pier and then descend near the crowds that gathered.

He traveled frequently to New York and must have been excited when in 1911 Cal Rodgers flew his Wright aeroplane from Sheepshead, New York, and landed in the water off Linden and Seaside in Long Beach just off the strand, not far from where John was standing. Someday he could take a flight.

A walk along this area allowed John to see the island of Catalina on the horizon and hear breakers twenty feet high or more crash across the same pier that had partially collapsed the year before.

It was a gruesome event. John and other residents from Scotland and England had been there, as had thousands of others, almost twenty-five thousand by some news accounts. All were celebrating Empire Day, or Queen Victoria's birthday, in daylong festivities arranged by the Sons of St. George for May 24.

The Sons of St. George were a local of a national group founded in Philadelphia in 1772 to assist those who had relocated from Britain. They arranged events to celebrate the British Empire and led most parades with Scottish bagpipes. The birthday of Queen Victoria was a particularly highly regarded celebration by expatriates.

A parade of men marched down Pine Avenue toward the pier and auditorium. Laughter and jubilance abounded. Hundreds of women, elderly men and children awaited them in front of the door of the auditorium, which remained locked.

Men marched along as the Kilter's Band played music from America and Lamb's beloved home, Scotland. The Scottish bagpipers had just entered the portal of the auditorium and were still marking time when the timbers were sundered, and a resounding crack sent an alarm through the throng that had gathered.

Ironically, the city would later defend itself of negligence by asserting that the pitch of the bagpipes resonated in the wood, causing a vibration so strong as to make the pier collapse.

THE CHICAGO SUNDAY TRIBUNE: MAY 25, 1913.

Auditorium at Long Beach, Where Collapse of Pier Killed or Injured Many.

PIER COLLAPSES;
33 ARE KILLED

EDNA KIMBALL BECOMES BRIDE.

Marriage to Henry H. Walt Takes Place at Sears Residence in

News article on the location of the collapse of the Long Beach Municipal Pier in 1913. *From the* Chicago Sunday Tribune, *May 25, 1913.*

In actuality, the collective weight of the hundreds awaiting the parade, added to the neglect by the city to maintain the girders beneath, caused the wooden deck floor to crumble and split open because of a rotted 4x14 girder that had been battered by sea water.

When the deck collapsed, bodies were thrown to the sand twenty feet below and crushed under the weight of other bodies and the splintered wood from the deck above. The screaming and moans were unbearable.

Those who fell into the hole last scrambled over the entangled bodies to the broken ends of the floor, so deep was it massed with struggling bodies. Falling timbers and flooring were jammed among the limbs of those caught in the trap and ropes were required to pull back the jagged edges of the sunken flooring and broken joists before the dead and injured could be taken out.

Dead and seriously injured alike were laid in rows on the sands of the beach in the midday sun, while scores who had sustained less serious injuries wandered dazedly about seeking missing relatives or friends. Many suffered from nervous shock.

It took considerable time for police to reach the victims because of the surging throng. The moans of the dying and shrieks of the injured and the panic-stricken filled the air. Those not caught up in the pier tried to give the survivors comfort as they were laid out on blankets in the sand, awaiting movement to the Long Beach Sanitarium, Seaside and St. Mary's Hospitals. Some were taken to the bathhouse emergency hospital, others to the Hotel Virginia nearby.

It was heartbreaking to walk on the sand and see the piles of eyeglasses, or rather spectacles, most of them of the strength usually required for older people. Some of them were broken, and others had the ear bows broken off. There were purses, bows, gloves and numerous hair switches and rats of every shade of color, most of them looking as if they had been torn roughly from the heads they adorned. There were nearly two hundred men's and boy's hats and caps of every shape, size and style ranging from Panama to cheap straws. Derbies were the most numerous and generally in a battered and mashed condition. Of women's headgear, there were hundreds of varieties of all shapes and styles, from cheap straws to everyday wear to dainty creations of lace or fashionable straw, the latter generally adorned with ostrich plumes.

Anyone who witnessed that horror no doubt could still see dozens and dozens of mangled bodies laid out on the sand. Most were women. A few old men and a child or two. The sight was devastating. A member of John's Bible class, Grace Helps, was crushed. Her husband passed away later on hearing of his wife's tragic death.

Next to bodies, there were piles of clothing, most of it torn from catching on the splintered deck. Shoes were still tied because they had been kicked

Inner view of floor collapse of Pine Avenue Pier. *From the* Los Angeles Times, *May 25, 1913.*

off. Cloaks, scarves, jackets, canes, hats and jewelry were stacked up so that families and those who survived could retrieve them.

If John walked the area on his way to the public comfort station, he could see the billboards of several of the theaters featuring plays like at the Bentley, "Amazons—The Tale of Women Performing the Deeds of Men," or at the Boston Theater featuring Cecil Engle, male impersonator.

While Long Beach had a reputation of being staid and dry, it also was the home of the new moviemaking industry beginning in 1910. The California Motion Picture Manufacturing Company opened a "movie plant" at Alamitos and Sixth and produced several moving pictures. It employed eleven actors and nine additional people. Interior scenes were shot at their studio, and the exterior scenes taken from real-life Long Beach and Signal Hill locations.

After the California Motion Picture Manufacturing Company left Long Beach in late 1912, it was replaced by the Edison Motion Picture Company, which only operated for six months. The company was producing "first aid" movies to be used by police. Motion pictures were seen as an opportunity to teach the growing immigrant population in the United States about "a respect for American law and order, an understanding of civic organization, pride in citizenship and in the American commonwealth," according to Lewis Jacobs's *Rise of the American Film: A Critical History*.

The Edison Motion Picture Company left Long Beach, and the property was then occupied by the Balboa Amusement Producing Company. The company produced films for William Fox and had a contract with author Jack London to produce motion pictures based on his writings.

The company's president, H.M. Horkheimer, praised Long Beach for its assets, calling it an "almost ideal locality for filming photodramas and comedies of all kinds" with:

> *wellnigh perpetual sunshine, its proximity to the ships and docks of San Pedro, the mountains and the seashore and the aid given the Balboa company by the people of Long Beach in granting permission for the use of houses, land and other background materials of all kinds utilized in the filming of photoplays.*

Balboa's first motion produced in 1913 Long Beach was the six-reel romance feature *St. Elmo*, from the 1866 southern novel written by Augusta J. Evans. The novel sold over four million copies. The studio produced eleven other motion pictures in the next twelve months with titles at the end stating that the motion picture was "Made in Long Beach."

To accommodate the growing motion picture industry, several theaters were added to the Long Beach Pike such as the Joyland theater, calling out the four-reel motion picture *The Spit Fire* being featured that day.

No one knows for certain why John Lamb took a detour from his walk that day. It was almost as if suddenly, he might have felt an overwhelming sense of loneliness and sadness that seemed to push him toward the open door of the public comfort station at Ocean Avenue at the foot of Locust, just five blocks from his beloved St. Luke's.

When John Lamb entered the comfort station, it was probably empty. This was Tuesday, and most visitors came here on the weekends or holidays. The station was most likely still clean and maintained. Had the station not been maintained, there would have been complaints published in the local newspaper as there had been about the other public comfort station near the auditorium.

When he entered, Lamb most likely saw a small lobby area and then an entrance to urinals inside a line of stalls with partitions between each. There should have been a janitor on duty on the men's side.

He would go into the stall that was sectioned off from the others and close the door. Men at that time wore suits and vests. Most were careful not to wear a red tie, because in some circles it signaled to other men that they were homosexual. Zippered pants had not yet arrived, so he would have to unbutton his suit pants and drop them to the floor and partially disrobe as he struggled with the union suit (long underwear) he wore underneath. If he wore the traditional union suit, he would then have to unbutton the flap in the back with a button and a "closed crotch" in the front. The more modern "Kenosha Klosed Krotch union suit" allowed a man to drop his suit pants and then draw apart the two pieces of body fabric overlapping like an *X*, pull out his penis and then relieve himself.

Eugene Fisher wrote to McClatchy, asserting:

> [Warren and Brown] *ply their game in public toilets…the comfort station at which they operated in Long Beach. They would watch until they saw a man who they thought to be given to this sort of thing and would attract his attention by putting their fingers through a hole in the board partition dividing the toilet walls. Upon looking through he would see a man's mouth close to the aperture and if he were that kind of man, and the suspicious* [sic] *of the officers correct, would stick his penis through the*

MEN'S FORM FITTING UNION SUITS.

SIZES: Give breast measure over vest close up under arms, and your height and weight.

A rational garment for men. Try our Union Suits for ease and comfort and you will wonder why you did not wear them before. Our Men's Union or Combination Suits fit. They are carefully and scientifically proportioned. We offer for your consideration only those suits that will fit, and we warrant them to be satisfactory in every particular.

80 Cents for $1.00 Men's Winter Weight Cotton Union Suits.

No. 16R6000 Men's Silver Gray Heavy Cotton Union Suits. Slightly fleeced on the inside, making them very soft and pleasant to the skin. Button down front. A special value at this low price. Finished neck and pearl buttons. Sizes, 34, 36, 38, 40, 42, 44. State breast, height and weight in your order.

Price, per dozen, $9.60; per suit.. ....80c

No. 16R6001 Men's Fine Union Suits, knitted from fine cotton yarn, same quality as the above, but in ecru color. Sizes, breast 34, 36, 38, 40, 42, 44. State height, weight and breast measure in order.

Price, each..............$0.80
Per dozen................ 9.60

If by mail, postage extra, each, 24 cents.

Sears Roebuck catalogue featuring union suit underwear for men. *Author's collection.*

hole, whereupon the officers would stamp his penis sometimes with indelible pencil and frequently with marker in some way and then run on upon him, arrest him and take him to the station.

Fisher told McClatchy that Warren claimed:

[Lamb] *not only put his private through giving an opportunity to brand him, but went into the next toilet compartment, where the detective was, in order that he might better accomplish his purpose. When they attempted to arrest him, he ran for several blocks, pursued by the officers, and finally fought them all over Pacific Park before they were able to land him at the station with clothes torn and hair disheveled.*

Lamb told his friends he had no idea that he was being accosted by law enforcement men or who the men might be.

He knew Pacific Park. It was just steps from St. Luke's. If he was sighted by anyone from the church, how could he explain why he was out of breath and looking like a vagrant who camped out on the beach? How could he explain who the men were just steps behind him?

Lamb and the church pastor, Reverend Bode, had just returned from representing St. Luke's at the annual convocation of the Los Angeles deanery at a boathouse at West Newport. The meeting focused on "How to Reach Scattered Members of the Denomination." The plan of work was for each clergyman and member of the vestry to visit parishioners in the little communities where there were no churches, each having the district around his own city. On Reverend Bode's list of visits with John were the towns of Hines, Clearwater, Compton, Willowbrook, Sativa and Lugo.

Shortly after that trip, John and two hundred members of St. Luke's celebrated the Reverend Bode's tenth wedding anniversary in the large room of the parish home. It was the last time John and L.H. sang together.

He could not overpower the two men who were dragging him to the city jail to appear before the police judge J.J. Hart, the same J.J. Hart who was the father of the man who just went camping for two weeks with his beloved L.H. Smith.

The two men restraining Lamb identified themselves to Police Court judge J.J. Hart as Special Officers W.H. Warren and B.C. Brown. They told Hart they caught Lamb in the public comfort station doing lewd acts and that they "had the goods on him." They showed Judge Hart the blue pencil mark made on Lamb, who objected, and told Judge Hart that the mark on his privates "was made by medicine he had used and asserted that he would explain later."

Lamb knew Hart was a "pioneer of Long Beach" and a former city trustee, a prominent citizen and the father of the man who had just camped with L.H. for two weeks.

Hart served on the city council for four years and two years as the justice of the peace. For the past seven years, he had served as Police Court judge. He conducted his court as he saw fit and often at the bidding of Mayor Whealton. The *Long Beach Telegram* referred to the "unwritten law of Judge Hart's Police Court."

Lamb had appeared before Hart two years earlier because he failed to have a light on the handle of his bicycle. Lamb was given a citation by the police and told he would need to pay a one-dollar fine to Judge Hart. When Lamb informed Hart he did not know it was against the law not to have a light on a bicycle, Hart admonished him that he would have known if he read the newspapers, which carried stories of new laws. John responded that he never read local newspapers and read only the *Los Angeles Times* each morning at breakfast. Hart made him pay the fine and directed him to start reading the local newspapers.

Now he stood before Hart protesting his innocence for a vile crime. Lamb resisted the report from Warren and Brown and yelled out, "As God is my witness, I have done nothing wrong."

Lamb was not the first brought before Hart by the special officers and probably not the last. And Judge Hart arraigned John Lamb as he did the others, without the presence of a defense attorney. Judge Hart found him guilty as charged and ordered that he pay $500 as bail in lieu of being jailed until trial.

Lamb asked to telephone his friend J.W. Tucker, who worked at John's bank. Tucker brought other friends, and they paid the bail so that John could go home.

Lamb was a broken man when he told Tucker and two other friends what had happened. His friends later told the newspapers that John was in a "terrible mental and broken condition," and they feared his despair would lead to him destroying himself if he were made to go to trial and have the details disclosed. They paid his bail and took him home.

His friends immediately contacted Mayor Whealton to make a complaint to the Police Commission about the horrible conduct of the two men who seized their friend at the public comfort station. They were denied a hearing and informed that the only way a protest could be made was if Lamb stood trial on the charges.

Judge Hart assured Lamb that if he pleaded guilty and paid the $500 as a fine, there would be no trial. (A $500 fine paid in 1914 is equivalent to about $14,840.40 today.)

After that day in September 1914, there is no mention in the local newspaper of John Lamb attending St. Luke's or any social event or traveling. Lamb did stay out of the press for almost two months.

John Lamb did not read the local press, so he had no idea what was taking place in Long Beach while he remained in seclusion. He had no idea how the political ambitions of several men would destroy him and ruin the lives of thirty other men.

EUGENE IRVING FISHER

LONG BEACH REPORTER FEEDS DETAILS TO *SACRAMENTO BEE*

There were other politically ambitious men in Long Beach besides Mayor Whealton, who especially understood the power of newspapers and their effect on political futures.

Eugene Irving Fisher was born in Minnesota in 1879. His family moved to Long Beach in 1896. He attended Berkeley for college and married Edna Moody from Long Beach.

In 1910, Eugene moved to Modesto, where the census listed him as an "Editor, local newspaper." He was elected one of the fifteen freeholders to write the charter for Modesto.

Fisher later lived in Sacramento, California, reporting for the *Sacramento Bee*, which is where he met publisher C.K. McClatchy. Eugene moved back to Long Beach in 1912 to work for the *Long Beach Press*.

He and his wife were named members of the Long Beach Old Settlers Club in 1914, a group that included Judge J.J. Hart and many other prominent persons who were considered the pioneers of Long Beach.

Whealton and Fisher were members of the same social circle in Long Beach. Both belonged to the City Club and served on committees directing its public policies.

Whealton opposed the appointment of freeholders to develop a new city charter that would include changing the form of government. Fisher wrote numerous articles for the *Long Beach Press* arguing against Whealton's positions and claiming that the change was necessary in Long Beach. Fisher pushed for a general manager form of government, which was used in the city of Berkeley, where he had lived.

Warren and Brown collected their ten dollars for collaring Lamb in September. They continued their efforts to find others of John Lamb's kind and to make more money.

Mayor Whealton was pleased with the efforts of the special officers, as the fines, reaching $5,275, assisted him in paying back the city treasury he had plundered.

The politically ambitious Whealton must have been upset that not one inch of ink was used by the local newspapers to print the details of the arrest of thirty-one degenerate men. How were the voters to know that he "ripped off the canker" and exposed such evil?

It would be too politically risky for Whealton to directly contact other newspapers, but he knew a Long Beach reporter and friend who could.

The timing of the contact between C.K. McClatchy and Eugene Fisher is not clear. The first story of the Long Beach arrests was published by the *Los Angeles Times* on November 14, 1914, as a result of Herbert Lowe's decision to demand a trial.

Fisher corresponded frequently with McClatchy, who was obsessed with Reverend Franklin Baker. Fisher answered McClatchy's questions and filed news stories about not only Long Beach but also Los Angeles. Fisher described the "depraved men and women" and how "it is growing and spreading like a hideous ulcer seeking with insidious arts and wiles ever to claim new victims among the boys and girls."

Eugene Fisher learned of these men's arrests and alleged activities through his connections with the Long Beach and Los Angeles police and a "young man whose name is known to Chief of Police Cole of Long Beach."

The young man described the practices of the Los Angeles "queers." He told Fisher:

Eugene I. Fisher, Who Was Made A Modesto Freeholder

COST OF LIVING RAISES SALARIES

OAKLAND, Aug. 1.—According to a report made today by County Superintendent of Schools Frick, the salaries of teachers have gone up during the

Eugene I. Fisher was selected as one of fifteen freeholders to draft the charter for the new city of Modesto. *From the* San Francisco Call and Post, *August 2, 1910.*

They are effeminate men on the whole and few busy men are found in their ranks. They call each other by endearing names and dress in women's clothing at their balls in Los Angeles. Their members include some of the wealthiest and most influential men of the city, so it is said, and the arrests that have been made lend credence to this statement.

Fisher claimed that the "young man" and police told him wild stories, stories about secret social clubs such as the "96 Club" where men allegedly dressed in female attire, silk kimonos, makeup and wigs and participated in orgies "without women." Fisher's news dispatches linked both Long Beach and Los Angeles arrests even though there was no proof of a connection. In doing so, he made the story of the Long Beach arrests even more significant.

McClatchy asked for names and locations, but Fisher could not provide any. He did, however, forward more salacious details of the events held, which he claimed were provided by the young man:

Disgusting in the extreme was a function described by this young social vagrant, himself not lost altogether to decency, which took place a few evenings ago in the richly furnished and perfumed apartments of a wealthy man in the heart of Los Angeles. Fourteen young men were invited to this party with the promise that they would have the opportunity of meeting some of the preeminent "queers" of the "Angel City" and the further attraction that some "chickens" as the new recruits in the vice are called, would be available. True enough some of the wealthy and prominent men of the city were there, politicians, prominent businessmen and every prominent churchmen. They were served an elegant repast and spent the evening in conversation and games of various sorts. Instead of place cards at each place was a candy representation of a man's privates which was sucked and enjoyed by each guest to the evident amusement of all. One or two of the young men were clad in women's clothing and entertained the gathering with music and song, it being stated that musicians, artists, and many gifted people of the professions are prone to this outrageous practice.

Fisher succeeded in inflaming McClatchy by including details of the sexual practices at the Los Angeles parties:

Nothing out of the way was attempted openly. But after most of the guests had gone the host asked one of his favorites to remain and then to the accompaniment of ragtime music played softly by the young man who was our informant as to the party, he executed his deed of depravity and satisfied his unnatural desire.

The young man told me that he has seen men, more or less under the influence of liquor at a function of that kind go around on their knees to various other persons present and attempt to "go down" on them right before the crowd and seemingly they have no shame about it.

Women were present as they also class themselves as "queer" and enjoy this "twentieth century way."

While Fisher never confirmed if the young man was telling the truth, he recounted to McClatchy that the young man stated there were "two thousand queers in Los Angeles alone"—a figure Fisher claimed was confirmed by police officers. He also added accounts of pedophilia:

Their number is constantly being recruited from among the boys and girls of well-to-do families, from the schools where the questions is becoming a serious one in every great city, and from the ranks of the poor, homeless newsboys on the street. God help them, with nobody to save them or warn them from the snares and pitfalls of these human vipers, vultures, and vampires.

McClatchy became determined not to let the local newspapers hide these "degenerates" as they had done with Reverend Baker.

Fisher cautioned McClatchy:

My dear C.K.
Use this in any way you see fit except as a signed article. As I said before, I would not care to sign it owing to the nature of the subject. As for the facts I have been exceptionally careful and I think you can rely on them. As sorry to have kept you waiting so long but it was a matter that could not be rushed. I still hope to secure the complete list with addresses and occupations from the Los Angeles office but is an uphill job like pulling eye teeth. The do not actually refuse, but they have a terribly complicated system of books and they will not give must assistance. I could not get anyone dependable that could get all the stuff thus far and have not had the time to dig it out myself with my other work. Have put a lot of time investigating the matter and trust you will find some of this available. Can give you more if you wish.

Sincerely,
Gene I. Fisher

P.S. What has made it so hard to get anything out of the Los Angeles office is this vice-probe of the City Prosecutor Geo. McKeeby, an account of which was contained in the Los Angeles Ex-amine [sic] Friday morning. It looks to me that Chief Sebastian and this city prosecutor now under fire have been protecting the big offenders and you can read that between the lines in the list of names I have sent. Perhaps you had better hold back the names until I have secured everything, I can get from the Los Angeles police office and then "shoot the wad."

The *Los Angeles Times* article about the Long Beach arrests and Lowe's request for a trial on November 14, 1914, began a publishing war in Northern and Southern California to see which newspapers could print the most salacious details and call out the hypocrisy of Long Beach for claiming it was better than other cities.

Tragically, the article would cause John Lamb to take his life.

12

HERBERT LOWE TRIAL RELEASES DETAILS OF "SPECIAL OFFICERS" ENTRAPPING LOCAL MEN

I t seemed everyone in Long Beach knew Herbert Lowe, the florist on Pine Avenue. Not only did Lowe provide the floral displays for most weddings, conventions and funerals, but he also often gifted the the *Long Beach Press-Telegram* with flowers to bedeck their offices.

Herbert was a man of medium build, with gray eyes and gray hair. Natives of Minnesota, Lowe and his family moved to the Long Beach area in 1899, when they bought a small tract of land in what was then the outskirts of the city and started a nursery, which later grew into an extensive florist's business. With the growth of the city, this land became part of a high-class apartment house district.

His mother served as president of the Alamitos Library Association, which raised funds for a new building.

According to a brief biography of Lowe in the 1936 edition of *Nautilus*:

> *Herbert Nelson Lowe developed an interest in shells in his high school days when he attended a series of classes in conchology given by Professor Josiah Keep at a local Chautauqua. During his years of active business life, he found time for collecting at near-by beaches, and by purchase and exchange built up a large collection. Vol. 13 of the* Nautilus, *1899, carried his first paper, the account of a dredging trip to Catalina Island, which secured a number of new species. A trip to Cedros Island, off the coast of Lower California, extended the known range of a number of California species southward.*

He worked in the Alamitos Nursery on Junipero and Elliot owned by his parents until they moved to Los Angeles in 1908. He remained in Long Beach and took over the nursery, and then he opened a floral shop in downtown Long Beach.

Herbert married Margaret Fitts, a teacher. The two of them became known for their involvement in community organizations. Margaret became the president of the Young Women's Christian Association and then the first president of the College Women's Club. Herbert served as an inspector at the polls during elections, and Margaret became involved in the Charter Amendment campaign to reform local government.

Lowe loved traveling, photography and shell collecting. He followed the Great White Fleet during its 1908 visit to Long Beach up the coast of California. When USS *New Jersey* sailed from Long Beach to San Francisco, two of its sailors were arrested on sodomy charges.

Lowe tracked the festivities in each of the towns the fleet ported, along with the magnificent floral displays set out to greet the fleet at each stop, and reported back to the local newspapers.

In late 1912, Herbert boarded a small ship called *The Flyer* and headed to the islands off the coast of Mexico. He was accompanied by Sergeant George Willet of the Los Angeles Police Department and W.J. McCloskey, a taxidermist, as part of the team commissioned by the county historical, science and art museum to gather specimens of the flora and fauna of the Mexican coast.

Lowe had been asked to join the trip because of his hobby of collecting shells from foreign lands and his expertise. This trip was the subject of an article in the *Nautilus*, a publication of the Academy of Natural Sciences of Philadelphia, which cited Lowe as a "high authority on conchology." As a result of donating his extensive collection of Cuban seashells to the Smithsonian Natural Museum, four of them were named in his honor. Later, he donated his entire molluscan collection to the San Diego Natural History Museum.

Lowe lived at 238 Junipero Avenue with his parents and wife. He turned a barn behind his home into a rental cottage.

The same month in 1914 that John Lamb was arrested, a man, who was later described in Lowe's trial as "young and feminine looking," stopped by Lowe's floral shop and made small talk. The conversation turned to the fact that the man, B.C. Brown, was looking to rent a room. Lowe offered to rent him his cottage behind his house near Broadway. Lowe did not know that the rent for the young feminine-looking man was paid by the Long

Mug shots of the two sailors from USS *New Jersey* arrested on charges of sodomy after the ship sailed from Long Beach. *San Francisco GLBT Historical Society.*

Beach police chief C.C. Cole as part of Mayor Whealton's secret plan to raise money by snaring men.

Herbert Nelson Lowe would be arrested and accused of being a "lewd vag" by the very same special officers who arrested John Lamb and twenty-nine other men. However, unlike the other men who were snared at the public comfort station by Warren and Brown, Lowe was arrested inside his own home. Of the thirty-one arrested, Lowe would be the first to plead not guilty and demand a jury trial to prove his innocence.

It was Lowe's trial and his alleged connection to a community of "social vagrants" that ignited the stories in the newspapers. Stories that printed the names of those men who had been arrested at or around the same time as Lowe. Stories that alleged that the men arrested were all members of "society of queers" and attended orgies where they dressed like women. Stories that included the name of James A. Lamb, "banker and churchman."

13

LOS ANGELES TIMES PUBLISHES DETAILS AND NAMES OF ARRESTED LONG BEACH SOCIAL VAGRANTS

Newspapers were not home delivered in 1914. In order to buy a copy of the *Los Angeles Times* on November 14, John Lamb would have to take a walk down to the Pacific Electric Railroad Station, where a group of newsies (newsboys) sold the newspapers.

The newsies were a growing group of poor or orphaned boys who made their living by buying newspapers in bulk and then hawking them at rail stations and other locations. They ranged in ages from five to thirteen.

John bought a newspaper and walked back to his home on Broadway. The front page was filled with stories of the war raging in Europe and the announcement of the withdrawal of American troops from Mexico.

The remainder of the paper featured advertisements, such as on page 5, which had a large advertisement for the Owl Drug Company:

> *Purity First. Yes, vitally so. The purity, the potency of any drug must satisfy us before it reaches you. The Owl spends many extra thousands of dollars to secure DRUGS OF PURITY. Every Owl Advertisement Is Filled with Pocket-Pleasing Surprises.*

Lamb left the pharmacy business just as it had started becoming dominated by large, impersonal drugstores.

Other major advertisements featured men's suits for eighteen dollars and "Manhattan shirts" for two dollars.

Poor young newsboys purchased newspapers in bulk and then sold them on the streets and at train stations to make a living. *National Child Labor Committee collection, Library of Congress, Prints and Photographs Division.*

The "Church" section on page 8 featured the schedule for the next day at St. John's Episcopal Church on Figueroa and West Adams. Lamb knew several of its members from conferences he attended for the Brotherhood of St. Andrew, an organization dedicated to bringing young men nearer to the teachings of Jesus. The rector, George Davidson, was speaking on "The Importance of the Individual" and "Our Citizenship Is in Heaven."

Page 4 had a curious article titled "Two Bachelors Desire Children." The article explained how two Chicago bachelors expressed that one of the great desires of their lives was to be surrounded by children. The men did not know each other, but somehow the reporter had found them. Both were men of means and good position and neither were married. The reporter claimed that the two bachelors, whom she would not name, admitted to her there are many men who look on marriage as "taking a chance with happiness but are wondering why they should be denied the pleasure of being surrounded by children." The current numbers of children left as orphans because of the war in Europe apparently prompted the article.

The last section of the newspaper included articles about cities other than Los Angeles. In the lower right of page 20 was the headline declaring:

Long Beach Uncovers "Social Vagrant" Clan. Thirty Men Heavily Fined or Given County-jail Sentences—Church and Businessmen Included in List of Guilty Ones Who Say They Have Evidence to Show, Were Organized Police Immoral Purposes.

LONG BEACH, Nov. 13—When Herbert N. Lowe, florist, and prominent citizen, was placed on trial today in Police Judge Hart's court on the charge of vagrancy, in that he was a "lewd and dissolute person," an astonishing story of a secret society of Long Beach men, termed "social vagrants," was unfolded by detectives who have been working on this and similar cases for more than two months.

The city treasury has been enriched by $5275 collected in fines in Police court from thirty citizens. Ten of these are now serving 180-day sentences in the County Jail. Some of the men fined are prominent in church work, one is a wealthy apartment-house owner, and several are merchants. Lowe was the only one of the thirty-one who pleaded not guilty.

It required eight hours of solid work to get a jury in the Lowe case today. Attorneys Swaffield & Swaffield, for the defendant, and the Deputy District Attorney exhausted almost all their peremptory challenges. Taking of testimony will be begun on Monday morning at 10 o'clock. The trial of the case is expected to take four days at least.

IMPORT STAR MEN. W.H. Warren and B.C. Brown, secret service men who have worked under Chief Sebastian of Los Angeles and who are now wearing Long Beach police stars, were engaged by Mayor Whealton and Chief of Police Cole to get evidence against a coterie of Long Beach men whose unnatural tendencies caused them to make advances to other men.

Warren and Brown have operated in the washrooms of the Long Beach bathhouse, in cottages, and elsewhere, getting evidence against these men. That they "produced the goods," is evident from the fact that thirty of those arrested paid fines in the last few days, ranging from $100 to $500, without a murmur.

According to Warren and Brown, Lowe was "easy" for them. Brown who is the younger of the "Special Officers" and has much the facial appearance of a young woman, tells the following story of Lowe's actions:

"I knew that Lowe had a house to rent in the rear of his residence at the corner of Broadway and Junipero streets. With the connivance of the Police Chief, I rented this cottage.

I kept strictly away from Lowe and the front house, but from the third day of my occupancy of the cottage he paid me early-morning visits. He would come over to surprise me at about 4 o'clock in the morning.

On the morning brazen and another officer were in the next room, with a peep hole which commanded a view of my bedroom, Lowe grew very brazen, and made proposals to me. He was caught by the officers as they burst in the room and was placed under arrest."

Assert He Confessed. Warren and Brown insist that Lowe made a full confession as soon as he arrived at the police station, stating, it is alleged by the two men, that he had been acting that way for about ten years. Lowe was expelled from a local secret order, it is stated, on account of his peculiar personality.

Lowe denies that he misconducted himself with Brown or Warren and insists that he was the victim of a "put-up job." He says that he had only friendly chats with Brown, in whom he took an interest. Lowe has been a resident of Long Beach for ten years.

Below Lowe's denial were a list of those arrested. There in black and white was John Lamb's name listed first among the other "social vagrants" and the fact that he was connected to a church:

The reports of "Special Officers" Warren and Brown and Judge Hart reveal a surprising array of convictions and fines of citizens on the same "social vagrancy" charge. Two prominent church men, John E. Lamb and J.A. Hayden, were fined $500 each. Other men who paid fines ranging from $100 to $300 were: C.C. Espey, F.K. Hinchings, L.E. Arnold, J.F. Storey, W.S. Austin, John Lain, Joseph Carran, W.J. Tronholm, George Grimes, E. Kessler, Roy Lyburger, Aref Said, J.W. Kerr, John Link, Albert Leidstrom, L.K. Flint, and W.J. McCandess. Those who received six months sentences in the County Jail are: Arthur Clarke, Robert Forbes, C.F. Edwards, P.L. Flaherty, W.L. Mean, Neis Bergfund, H.C. Kerlin, George Graham, W.R. Berry and Fred Long.

Offers To Peach? Officers Warren and Brown say that Lowe unfolded to them before his arrest a story of the existence of a society of "social vagrants," called the "606," whose members were all men and who met weekly. He offered to take the officers to the place, according to Warren's story. At the functions of this peculiar society all the members, on arriving, changed street clothes for kimonos, silk underwear and hosiery, and some wore women's wigs. The members made up with powder and paint as for the stage, according to the recital of the officers, and the orgies were attended by at least fifty at each meeting. Lowe asserts he made no such confession and that he said nothing about a secret society.

Chief of Police Cole is a witness in the case against Lowe, as are several of his men. Mayor Whealton, Chief of Police Cole, and Judge Hart have caused to be issued a written recommendation of the work of Warren and Brown, stating, over their signatures, that the men have "rid the city of a dangerous class which threatened the morals of the youth of the community." Many people think political vengeance is at the bottom of it all.

But what a holy city Long Beach is!

The thought that his sister or anyone he knew at St. Luke's or the bank would learn of the horrible crime for which he was accused that linked him to "a dangerous class which threatened the youth of the community," must have horrified Lamb. He had chosen not to have a trial when arrested, but with his name in the newspaper, Lamb was now undergoing a trial in the court of public opinion.

Lamb moved quickly after reading the morning news. He took the newspaper and carefully wrote Marion's name and their address on the side of the newspaper, which he would leave where he committed the deadly deed. He then tucked it into his coat pocket and headed out to the Pacific Electric trolley nearby to go to San Pedro and Point Fermin.

14

ONLY ONE NEWSPAPER PRINTS LAMB'S ENTIRE SUICIDE NOTE

John Lamb's lifeless body was discovered by two women from Long Beach who were on an early morning outing, Mrs. F.E. Grossley of 2646 Vermont Avenue and her sister, Mrs. Dunbar. Coincidently, the women recognized Lamb. They notified men who were nearby who in turn telephoned the police. The men reported that they had found a "floater" in the water near the rocks, thinking that he may have drowned.

Officer Dunn responded and arranged for Lamb's body, which was badly bruised by his falling among the rocks, to be taken to Booth Mortuary in San Pedro. Later, his body was claimed by family and friends. Dunn reported Lamb had a vial in his hand and was clutching the newspaper in another. A note to his sister lay next to his body.

The newspapers that would carry the details of Lamb's death conjectured that Lamb had found an old postcard among the rocks and scribbled his suicide note to his sister shortly before taking the poison. It is highly unlikely that Lamb waited until arriving at Point Fermin to pen a note to his sister, as he had so carefully written her name and address on the *Los Angeles Times* before leaving Long Beach. Most likely, because the postcard appeared dirty and old, the reporters assumed it Lamb had found it among the rocks that morning.

John Lamb's suicide was front-page news by the early evening editions of most local newspapers. Later, the story spread across the United States through Associated Press. The Long Beach and San Pedro newspapers carried headlines on the front page, shouting:

LIFELESS BODY FOUND ON ROCKS—At Point Fermin, with Empty Cyanide Vial Nearby—Leaves Scribbled Note to Sister

SLAYS SELF ON READING "EXPOSE"—John A. Lamb Takes Dose of Poison at Early Hour This Morning at Point Fermin. NOTE TO SISTER ASSIGNS REASON. Tragedy Outgrowth of News Account of Long Beach Crusade on Alleged "Vice Ring."

SUICIDE FOLLOWS THE LONG BEACH EXPOSE—Prominent Church Worker and Prohibitionist Who Paid $500. Fine Committed Suicide at Pt. Firmin This Morning—Unfortunate Man Could Not Stand the Disgrace and Ended His Trouble with Poison, Left Note Declaring His Innocence. Nearly Every Man Who Paid the Fines and Those in the

Point Fermin Lighthouse stands atop the steep bluff. *Public domain. University of Southern California Libraries and California Historical Society.*

County Jail Have Been Active in Civic Uplift and Prohibition and the Expose Came as a Distinct Shock to Their Friends as Did the Suicide This Morning.

Exposure of Bizarre Orgies Causes Suicide. Unable to Bear Shame, Wealthy Church Member of Long Beach Takes Poison—Thirty Men Fined or Sentenced—Participants in Orgies Dressed as Women in Kimonos.

Long Beach Uncovers "Social Vagrant" Clan. Thirty Men Heavily Fined or Given County-Jail Sentences—Church and Businessmen Included in List of Guilty Ones Who, Police Say They Have Evidence to Show, Were Organized for Immoral Purposes. The News Reprints the Following Story, Not as an Item of News Because the Facts Have Been Known for over Two Years, But as a Rebuke to Certain "Holy of Holies" in Long Beach Who Have Used San Pedro as an Example of Vice and Lawlessness—Vultures, Human as Well as the Cleaner Kind of Air, Invariable Come Home to Roost.

While all the newspapers printed some of the contents of the note left for Lamb's sister, only the *San Pedro Pilot* included the entire note, in which Lamb named L.H. Smith as "doing this":

My Darling Sister: God knows and will have mercy through Christ. I am crazed by reading the paper this morning. I never knew of such orgies. I am innocent but the victim of a situation. I could not endure this publicity as I had no chance to deny it.

Go to the office and Mr. Tucker will act as your advisor. The Third Street property is yours by deed. Have it recorded.

Believe me innocent. How I love you both, but it is best. Be brave. Your friends and mine will believe. I think L.H. Smith is doing this.

John.

One newspaper deleted reference to L.H. and printed that "blank was doing this." Nothing further was ever reported concerning Lamb's allegations against L.H. Smith, nor was he ever named in Long Beach newspapers as being connected with Lamb.

After John Lamb's body was taken to a San Pedro mortuary it was claimed by two friends, Charles Tucker, a cashier at Lamb's bank and the person named in his suicide note who would take care of his sister, and Percy Smith, the brother of L.H. The two men helped transfer his body to the J.J. Mottell Morgue in Long Beach.

Official death certificate of John Amos Lamb. *Los Angeles County Records.*

Six days after Lamb's death in San Pedro, the local newspaper carried these headlines on its front page: "Social Vagrant Convicted Here, Long Beach Has No Monopoly on Vice; Oscar Wilson Convicted." The story mentioned John Lamb's suicide and the fact there had been no publicity of his arrest prior to his death.

Evening editions of newspapers all over the nation carried the wire service story of Lamb's suicide and his connection with the list of other "social vagrants."

Claiming that another man on the published list had threatened suicide that same day, the Long Beach health officer, Ralph Taylor, and Police Chief Cole ordered local pharmacists to stop dispensing poisons. The order allowed:

Milder portions can be sold without a physician's permit. The stronger and more deadly poisons such as cyanide of potassium, prussic acid, and strychnine and arsenic can be secured only by the presentation of a physician's certificate calling for the use of the portions for medical purposes.

The ban on the sale of these poisons was lifted in one day.

On Monday, the judge paused the Lowe trial because of Lamb's suicide and the illness of one of the jurors.

Even though John Lamb was a devout member of St. Luke's Episcopal Church, he would be denied burial rites at St. Luke's by Anglican rules. Taking one's life was a sin, a blasphemy against God, and a blessed funeral was denied to those who took their own life.

Friends of John Lamb were quick to tell reporters of his innocence. They penned a lengthy article for the San Bernardino newspapers and were quoted by others. They claimed that while on a visit to the public comfort station, John,

out of curiosity, became involved in the dragnet of the "Special Officers" placed on the trail of vagrants of vice. Rather than submit to the publicity of a trial, he pleaded guilty and paid the heavy fine.

They also declared that "political vengeance" was at the bottom of the work of the detectives, but they did not provide further details and never mentioned L.H. Smith.

The Long Beach special officers Warren and Brown responded in the newspaper that every one of the thirty-one names contained in their report were unquestionably guilty of the charges brought against them.

The newspapers also published the alleged police blotter record of the arrest of John Lamb to prove his guilt. The record contained an incorrect age for Lamb, who just seven days prior to his suicide had turned fifty-two years old:

John A. Lamb, aged 40 years, native of Scotland, in the United States twenty years, in California eighteen years, and in Los Angeles county twelve years. Arrested September 22, 1914, on a charge of vagrancy; pleaded guilty in Police Court before Judge J.J. Hart, and paid a fine of $500; arrested by "Special Officers" Warren and Brown at the Long Beach Bath-House comfort station.

While his friends prepared for John's burial, more and more newspapers spread the story of his suicide and the scandal he had hoped to avoid:

LONG BEACH ROCKED BY SCANDAL. "Six Hundred and Six" Case Threatens to Wreck Homes. Suicide of Banker is the Climax to Operations of Weird Club.

SOCIAL VAGRANT TAKES OWN LIFE. Wealthy California Man Prominent Churchman, Kills Self on Beach. POISON SALE STOPPED. Fearing Suicide of Others Involved with John Lamb, Long Beach Police Ban Poison Sale Altogether.

LONG BEACH SCANDAL RENEWED BY A SUICIDE. The Club to Which Franklin Baker Belonged Again Involved.

Long Beach.

LONG BEACH UNCOVERS "SOCIAL VAGRANT" CLAN.

Thirty Men Heavily Fined or Given County-jail Sentences—Church and Business Men Included in List of Guilty Ones who, Police Say They Have Evidence to Show, were Organized for Immoral Purposes.

[LOCAL CORRESPONDENCE.]

LONG BEACH, Nov. 13.—When Herbert N. Lowe, florist and prominent citizen, was placed on trial today in Police Judge Hart's court on the charge of vagrancy, in that he was "a lewd and dissolute person," an astonishing story of a secret society of Long Beach men, termed "social vagrants," was unfolded by detectives who have been working on this and similar cases for more than two months.

The city treasury has been enriched by $5275 collected in fines in Police Court from thirty citizens. Ten of

a view of my bedroom, Lowe grew very brazen, and made proposals to me. He was caught by the officers as they burst in the room and was placed under arrest."

ASSERT HE CONFESSED.

Warren and Brown insist that Lowe made a full confession as soon as he arrived at the police station, stating, it is alleged by the two men, that he had been acting that way for about ten years. Lowe was expelled from a local secret order, it is stated, on account of his peculiar propensity.

Lowe denies that he misconducted himself with Brown or Warren, and insists that he was the victim of a "put-up job." He says that he had

McClatchy touts large-scale "social vagrancy" scandal in Southern California. *From the Sacramento Bee, November 16, 1914.*

Because the Episcopal Church forbade church services for one who died by suicide, John could not have funeral services inside the church. The services were held on November 16, 1914, at the home he shared with his sister Marion at Coronado and Broadway in east Long Beach.

Many friends attended. The Reverend Arnold Bode, pastor of the church, for whom John had sung his last solo, officiated at services in the Lamb home along with the two former rectors of the church, Revered Charles T. Murphy and the Reverend Robert Gooden.

Even though Long Beach had a large municipal cemetery, John's sister Marion chose to have him

Headstone of John Amos Lamb and his sister Marion, who died in 1930. *Angelus-Rosedale Cemetery.*

buried in Angelus-Rosedale Cemetery in Los Angeles. The pallbearers, who were vestrymen from St. Luke's, took his coffin and laid him to rest. Angelus-Rosedale is located on a slope in the southwestern part of Los Angeles. It was the area's first cemetery to allow burials of persons of every race and religion and the resting place for many politicians.

15

GENDER IMPERSONATION IS ALL THE RAGE IN LONG BEACH

The newspapers continued to include John Lamb's suicide in all their accounts of Herbert Lowe's trial. However, the reporters were not fastidious with fact-checking the details. Some referred to him as "John A. Lamb" and others as "John E. Lamb." One newspaper published his name as "John C. Land." His age was listed as ranging from thirty-five to forty-two, when in fact he was fifty-two. Some stated he died taking "carbolic acid," and others noted he drank "potassium of cyanide."

The newspapers also wrote that thirty-one men were arrested in Long Beach as "social vagrants," while others expanded that number to fifty.

Most articles erroneously lumped together all the men arrested, including Lamb, as being members of a "immoral society" that frequented the "606 Club" (which was sometimes referred to as the "69 Club"), where they allegedly wore wigs, makeup, kimonos, silk underwear, hosiery and slippers and engaged in orgies "without women."

Several newspapers added sensational details of the activities that allegedly occurred at the 606 Club to include "a queer altar, before which its weird rites were performed."

The *Pomona Daily Review* even alleged that the governor of California won a majority of votes in Long Beach because the "606 club was in full operation there." No facts were ever substantiated that such a club existed.

These stories developed during Lowe's trial: Special Officers Warren and Brown alleged that Lowe had told them of the details of the "secret 606

Club" and Lowe had invited them to take Brown for a visit. Some of the newspapers dismissed the existence of such a club altogether. Its location was never disclosed.

Eugene Fisher's articles were published by McClatchy without a byline and used to attack Long Beach as "the home of a secret society of degenerate men, bearing a remarkable name." The *Bee* also featured an anonymous letter to the editor, published on the front page, thanking the newspaper for running the articles on the Long Beach scandal. The letter was most likely written by Fisher.

Most newspapers were reluctant to elaborate on what the arrested men did at their supposed meeting places. McClatchy, through Fisher, filled in the scandalous details:

A. B. Hill: "No wonder Hiram Johnson had 2600 majority in Long Beach; they had that 606 club in full operation there."

Abe Skinner: "People probably don't talk about you behind your back as

Political quip alleging large amount of "social vagrants" from Long Beach voted to elect Hiram Johnson governor of the state. *From the* Pomona Daily Review, *November 18, 1914.*

On certain gala nights the men would come to their meeting place, array themselves in kimonos, loosely hung from the shoulders, put on silk stockings, French heeled slippers, rouge their faces and then proceed to the revels, which have resulted in the quiet payments of fines or submissions to long jail terms with as little publicity as possible. Some of the men even wore women's wigs. The members made up as for the stage.

Behind the scenes, Fisher egged on McClatchy in his notes:

Arrests have been going on quietly for years both here in Long Beach and Los Angeles, the officers inform me, and with very little publicity. I suppose Long Beach would not have been given the unusual publicity had not The Times in its usual manner, sought to hold this municipality up to scorn for being such a "holy city."

More than 2,000 social vagrants, moral degenerates and sodomites are plying their infamy in Los Angeles alone, according to a statement by a young man to a reporter for The Bee and an officer of the law, who has been a habitus of the "96" Clubdom.

Nightly orgies are held by social vagrant clubs, "96" organizations and "queers" in the very heart of Los Angeles when unspeakable crimes are perpetrated upon mere boys and practices are resorted to so loathsome and degrading that they would have put the blush to the very Cities of the Plains.

Whether or not some of the men are innocent, we probably can never know, but this is certain that this damnable practice is being carried on in Long Beach, in Los Angeles and in every city today. It flourishes in the public toilets and in the parks and if it is not held down by the heavy hand of the law, these professional "social vagrants" brazenly seek their victims on the streets and in the parks and places where men and boys congregate. Almost every man or boy seems to have encountered it in some place or other during his life.

Ironically, men who impersonated women were a growing phenomenon and a public fascination in 1914. Months before the exposé of the "96" and "606 Club," Long Beach newspapers carried half-page articles with photographs of the popular female impersonator, dubbed "the queerest woman in the world," Julian Eltinge.

Born William Julian Dalton, Eltinge played the "Fascinating Widow" and the "Crinoline Girl" in popular vaudeville shows. These performances included him wearing elaborate dresses, makeup and a wig, complete with staging and dancing.

Supporters were quick to note:

Eltinge is a thorough gentleman at all times with no trace of effeminacy about him and has always dignified his performances with artistic methods.

The year before the arrests, Long Beach newspapers announced sold-out performances of Lazar, "a clever female impersonator" at the Bentley-Grand Theater on the Pike.

In fact, several female impersonators performed at live theaters along the Pike: "Carless" at the Byde-a-Whyle, "Divine Dobson" at the Boston and "Harry Allister" at the Orpheum. Reporters noted that these female impersonators wore the finest of garments that would "make any woman jealous."

The same month Lamb was arrested, Long Beach newspapers carried advertisements about "Miss Cecil Engle," a "male impersonator" performing at the Boston on the Pike, pointing out:

It is quite an unusual occurrence to have the female impersonator as an act, but the impersonation of the opposite sex is something just a little out of the ordinary and again demonstrates that in this age the gentler sex does not intend to be outdone by man "Long live the suffragettes."

Julian Eltinge in one of his many costumes. *Library of Congress.*

Again, newspapers were careful to note that impersonators, like Engle, kept their sexual identity during their performance:

> *Cecil Engle, a vivacious piece of femininity, entertains charmingly with her clever male impersonations that have won her fame from coast to coast.*

Wearing the clothing of the opposite sex in public was against the law. Police explained that if a man dressed like a woman or a woman dressed like a man, the police would not be able to identify criminals. In Germany in the early 1920s, police gave cards to those who engaged in "transvestitism" indicating the police had checked them and knew their correct gender.

Long Beach residents were not as outraged by the allegations of what occurred in the so called "96" or "606 Club" as they were that John Lamb, a prominent man many knew, took his life because the *Los Angeles Times* published his name.

16

LONG BEACH MINISTERS OUTRAGED BY LAMB SUICIDE, DEMAND PUBLISHER STOPS BRUTAL JOURNALISM

S everal ministers and members of the Long Beach Chamber of Commerce condemned the publication of the details of the Lowe case and the several newspapers that had sensationalized the details as "being unprintable."

The ministers and businessmen threatened to confront General H.G. Otis, publisher of the *Los Angeles Times*, and "demand that he publishes no more articles on crime in Long Beach," as the articles were ruining the city's reputation.

Otis would not stop and wrote a scathing editorial on November 21, just days after John Lamb's burial:

> CLEANING UP LONG BEACH. *The action of Mayor Whealton and those associated with him in seeking to purge Long Beach of these men who are accused of setting up in our beautiful suburb a twentieth century Sodom cannot be too highly commended. A morality mephitic atmosphere is as deadly to clean social life as if the yellow fever to physical health. Both are symotic diseases, to be driven away only by cleaning—is the one case the hearthstones, in the other the gutters. Suicide is never a sane resort from the consequences of crime, unless the person accused is guilty, and if guilty death or flight is a duty he owes to his friends and*

the community he has dishonored. Suicide is not absolute proof of guilt or a confession of guilt, although it is generally considered as both. No man can clear his records by suicide, and no man who believes in an existence after death will, if in his right mind, expect to avoid disgrace by taking his own life.

If it were a common practice for a man, who by crookedness and exhibition of debauched moral sense, had caused his fellow-citizens to regard him as a moral pariah, to partly expiate his ill doing by suicide, The Times would wonder that a certain newspaper proprietor in Los Angles had not long ago climbed the golden stair, or rather descended the asbestos ladder, and been assigned by his friend the devil to a berth close to the furnace. He would have committed suicide long ago if he had any sensitiveness [sic] or conscience.

Publicity is a better preventive of such crimes as are now in progress of investigation at Long Beach than a morbid suppression of them. The higher the social station of those accused the more imperative the duty of turning the searchlights of the press upon them. There is no danger of innocent men being harmed by investigation.

When upon good evidence an arrest is made it is the duty of a newspaper to print the fact of the arrest and the evidence which warranted it, as news, and no namby pamby bleating of rival and "scooped" journals have ever diverted or ever shall prevent The Times from giving the news to its readers. In printing such news, it is not necessary to give filthy details or to print anything that may not be read in the family circle. When it is said that the accused was charged with the same crime as that for which Sodom was destroyed and Oscar Wilde was imprisoned, or that he was accused of contributing to the delinquency of a minor female, or of misconduct with a child, the mature reader understands without the aid of a dictionary exactly what is meant and no law of decency is offended.

Of course, there are newspaper proprietors—The Times has one in view—who could not keep themselves clean while sweeping out a gutter, no matter how long the handle of the broom they wielded. They would be sure to sit down in any cesspool that chanced to be open. Of course, these journalistic degenerates and hypocrites are always opposed to any exposure of degeneracy and hypocrisy.

If, as a result of the Long Beach investigation, the accused, or any of them, shall not be conclusively proven guilty, The Times will be more than glad to make public their innocence. If convicted, it will be equally ready to chronicle their guilt. The Times is sure that Mayor Whealton will do

his whole duty without favor and without fear, and it commends him for his
zeal in taking measures to ascertain the truth.

Lowe's attorney Roland Swaffield deflected the condemnation of Lamb by telling jurors during the trial that the "blood of John Lamb was dripping" from the hands of Special Officers Warren and Brown, the same two who had snared his client.

Mayor Whealton staunchly defended Lamb's arrest and claimed again that Lamb admitted his own guilt when he pleaded guilty and paid the fine. Whealton was quoted in the *Los Angeles Times* as saying:

> *The police department has started to clean up the town, and we proposed to clean it up, regardless of the protests. We are not through yet. There are other sore spots needing attention.*
>
> *I am in favor of publishing these cases. Open the canker, and let the rottenness out, and then we have a chance to be well again. We can gain nothing by suppressing the truth concerning these men.*
>
> *I resent the allegations by friends of Lamb, recently published, that he was told he would be let off easy if he would plead quietly. We had evidence of Mr. Lamb's misconduct, and an attorney and two friends came here and demanded a Police commission inquiry. We told them Mr. Lamb must go before the court and be dealt according to law.*

Judge Hart told the newspapers:

> *John A. Lamb was guilty of the charge of vagrancy as any of the group, although we all deplore his death. Mr. Lamb confessed his guilt at the time he appeared before me. I have known for some time of the guilt of this defendant, and it has been of knowledge to other men.*
>
> *I am in favor of publishing the names and acts of these degenerates. Let the cases be sent broadcast, printed in huge letters, and show up the wickedness. Publicity for these kinds of cases is the greatest aid to the suppression of the vice.*

McClatchy sent Fisher a typed note asking if Lamb confessed and why Lamb would be in such a "filthy place." Fisher responded:

> *According to Chief Cole, Lamb never actually confessed. He told Hart, when asked what the mark on his privates meant, which Warren and*

Brown assert they placed there…that the blue pencil mark was made by medicine he had used and asserted that he would explain later. Judge Hart says he never came back to explain but that his attorney, Geo. Skinner, came and paid his fine.…He also declared that detectives rushed in upon him and dragged him to court for something he knew not what.

The publishers of Sacramento, San Pedro and Los Angeles newspapers continued to seize this scandal as an opportunity to publicly chastise Long Beach for hypocritically acting as if it were a "holy city" and that other cities were corrupt.

Days after John Lamb was buried, E.T. Earl, the publisher of the *Los Angeles Tribune* and *Evening Express* and a fierce competitor of the *Los Angeles Times*, wrote the following editorial in response to the news articles which precipitated Lamb's suicide:

JOURNALISM THAT IS SO BRUTAL THAT IT KILLS.

Brutal journalism sometimes becomes homicidal journalism. Several instances are supplied by the recent record of local events. Driven to desperation because they were made the victims of sensational publicity, men have sought refuge in death from the attacks that were made upon them. They preferred to meet the instant judgment of God rather than face the merciless clamor of men.

It is the business of newspapers to print the news, but that duty should be performed in decency and with discrimination. No man is so well fortified in the respect and regard of the community, by even a lifetime of good conduct, as to be immune against causeless attack. It is within the power of any abnormal person actuated by malice, moved by blackmail or stirred merely by a love of sensationalism, to bring accusations of a frightful character. Such charges ought not to be given publicity until proof of their truth has formally been adduced. Otherwise, an irreparable injury is inflicted even upon the wholly guiltless.

Official portrait of Edwin Tobias Earl, founder and publisher of the *Los Angeles Evening Express. Los Angeles Public Library Digital Collections.*

No interest of society is subserved by the premature exploitation of such accusations. The public will be as well protected against the offender if publicity is withheld until conviction shall have been secured. The adoption of such a policy would spare the victims of false witness the frightful shame and unendurable disgrace that now so often permanently attaches itself to the accused even when acquitted. Sometimes it happens that men of high spirit and extreme sensitiveness, unable to endure the reflection that they have been held up to public scorn, take their lives rather than to face, even though innocent, the biting contempt of a censorious world too prone to give prejudgment on insufficient evidence.

It should not only be the policy of decent newspapers to withhold publication of charges affecting honor and character until there shall have been a legal adjudication of guilt or innocence, but public officials themselves should exercise a superior discretion in dealing with cases of this nature. Morbidity that finds gratification in publicity, abnormal natures that are in fact affected with psychic disturbances, blackmailers ever seeking to find victims—all these go in endless procession to the offices of public officials with tales and accusations that ought not to be the basis of public official action except after the most rigid and exacting inquiry.

The character of an honorable man is dearer to him than his physical life. His good name is esteemed by him as is his most precious possession, and accusations of infamy, supported by official proceedings based thereon, and reinforced by the publicity given by a sensational newspaper, inflict a strain that never can be eradicated. The world should act upon the principle that the accused is innocent until he is proved guilty.

Let us have an end of the wicked, cruel system that now obtains and begin here a reformation that will reach in its influence to the uttermost extent of the Union. Guilt must be punished! True, but punishment of the guilty is not endangered by withholding publicity until proof makes it certain that innocence takes no injury.

Los Angeles Times publisher Otis retaliated against Earl by printing a column that later resulted in a defamation lawsuit filed by Earl:

DEFENSE OF DEGENERATES.
The theory of the editor of the Morning Sodomite and the Evening Degenerate seems to be that those who violate the laws of God and man should be protected from punishment and sheltered from publicity, while those newspapers whose proprietors publish the news, and by so doing

aid decent people to avoid ignorantly contaminating their households with well-dressed, cultivated Pharisaical moral lepers, are to be denounced as "brutal journalists."

The too pious system is to coddle criminals, to conceal their crimes, and to denounce those who expose crime as "brutal journalists." The system of the Times *is to publish the news, and if the news includes an account of the misdoings of a lot of pretentious Pharisees, who are as lecherous as goats and as conscienceless as jackasses in April, the acts of the evil-doers will be exposed, notwithstanding the purchased defense of the editor of the Morning Sodomite and Evening Degenerate.*

Civil War brigadier general Harrison Gray Otis, publisher of the *Los Angeles Times. UC Berkeley, Bancroft Library.*

Fisher sent McClatchy a handwritten note encouraging that he:

dig into The Times *for playing up degeneracy in Long Beach and saying nothing about it in Los Angeles. I meant to bring that out in my stories but forgot. The L.A. papers have hardly more than mentioned their own deplorable condition. Clear case of spite against "Holy City" of Long Beach.*

The publisher of the *Sacramento Bee* continued his fixation on the Long Beach "scandal," in a large part due to his being outraged by the earlier non-prosecution of Reverend Baker. He wrote a lengthy editorial titled "Publicity Is Needed; And Then More Publicity."

One newspaper in that section published what it decently could of the facts concerning the male "social vagrants" of Long Beach, Los Angeles County, and gave their names.

Because one man who protested his innocence committed suicide, the other papers, which failed in their duty in the way of publishing the legitimate news concerning this horrible offense, have worked a few church and kindred people to public declarations against "scandal papers," "articles of vicious character," and to demanding a "campaign for decency."

It must be remembered that the Long Beach man who committed suicide, subsequently to professing his innocence, previously had admitted his guilt, and been fined most heavily. More than that: His suicide itself was a confession.

McClatchy also included misleading information as to how he obtained information from Long Beach. Instead of acknowledging that he was using a former *Sacramento Bee* reporter, he wrote:

There are some people In Los Angeles County thoroughly ashamed of this shameful policy of suppression. One of these has written to The Bee from Long Beach. His letter shows the infamy and the spread of this social vagrancy and he says I wish to say I am glad one newspaper man in the United States stands ready to throw the light of publicity on these cases. This is certain that this damnable practice…flourished…and if it is not held down by the heavy hand of the law, these professional social vagrants seek their victims.…Owing to the nature of the subject, I do not care to have my name attached to any article; but in the cause of humanity, I am only too glad to furnish anything I can in the way of information regarding the degeneracy question, as I find it in the community and in Los Angeles.

The statement was verbatim from the notes exchanged with Fisher prior to McClatchy's column.

While newspaper publishers fought over what was appropriate to print about the men arrested in Long Beach, Herbert Lowe's floral shop remained busy. These supporters were quick to agree that Lowe was "the victim of stoolpigeons" hired by city hall. Swaffield's defense strategy was working.

The city did not have its own court building, so the council chambers had to serve as a courtroom. The council debated about building a second story on the city hall so that trials could be conducted there. The city hall was often referred to as "old, ramshackle, antedated, antiquated" and considered a "fire trap" because of its wooden structure. Because the city government had expanded, the city had to rent an "annex" to house officials.

There was growing concern that should the building catch on fire, all city records would be destroyed. Some called for a bond issue to finance a reinforced-concrete building, which would provide more room for municipal offices and the police.

But for the time being, residents had to fight to get a seat at the Lowe trial and paid one dollar to men who had arrived early to sell their seats. There was no lack of takers, even though it was rumored that the complete details of why Lowe was arrested would be revealed only in the judge's closed chambers.

The trial was repeatedly delayed because several of the jurors asked to be excused on account of illness. It was difficult finding replacements for those who had not read the *Los Angeles Times*' account of the scandal and who had not already formed an opinion.

One juror had to be dismissed when it was discovered he had been deemed "insane" by the "Lunacy Commission" and sent to Patton State Hospital the prior year. The same juror was overheard in a local pool hall saying that Lowe was not guilty. The juror was finally dismissed after "conducting himself in a queer manner, fixing his gaze upon Lowe for minutes," reported the *Los Angeles Times*.

To make matters worse, the remaining jurors found newspapers in their seats after returning from recess. The newspapers contained "startling accounts of the case." Lowe's attorney moved to dismiss the case.

The trial was also postponed when the prosecutor could not locate his key witnesses, Special Officers Warren and Brown. Both were needed to give details of the "606 and 96 clubs" and to explain how they marked

Long Beach City Hall where Herbert Lowe's trial was held. *Author's collection.*

NOTICE TO CREDITORS.
Estate of John A. Lamb, Deceased.
Notice is hereby given by the un-
dersigned, the executrix of the estate
of John A. Lamb, deceased, to the
creditors of, and all persons having
claims against the said deceased, to
exhibit the same with the necessary
vouchers, within 10 months after the
first publication of this notice to the
said executrix at the office of her attorney, Geo. A. Skinner, rooms 403-4
Long Beach National Bank building,
in Long Beach, in the County of Los
Angeles, being the place designated
for the transaction of the business of
this estate.
Dated this 3rd day of December,
A. D. 1914.
MARION J. LAMB,
Executrix of Said Estate.
GEO. A. SKINNER,
Attorney for the Estate.
(D3—J3)

Probate notice for the estate of John A. Lamb. *From the* Long Beach Press Telegram, *December 8, 1914.*

the bodies of those they arrested with "the secret indelible mark 'S.S.'" or a cross.

Lowe's attorney again moved for dismissal. Judge S.H. Underwood ruled in early December that Lowe would have a new trial and issued summons to one hundred to be interviewed for a new jury panel of twelve.

Few male residents wanted to serve on the jury. No women were called to jury service. Even though women were given the vote in 1911 in California, they were excluded from serving on juries in until 1917, when state law was passed. That right was challenged in 1918 by a man being tried for rape who argued that women could not fairly hear the case. However, the California Supreme Court affirmed that women had a constitutional right to serve on juries. Because Lowe was especially popular with women, it was thought that there would be no problem obtaining a not-guilty verdict.

As the new trial was set, legal notices were printed in the local newspapers by John Lamb's sister Marion as executrix of his estate. She was moving forward to probate his will and settle any debts he may have acquired before his death.

17

HERBERT LOWE WINS AND OTHER NAMED SOCIAL VAGRANT DEMANDS TRIAL

H erbert Lowe was not the only one of the thirty-one arrested who decided to protest his innocence by demanding a trial. Charles E. Espey, whom newspapers referred to as "a wealthy retired art dealer," was arrested by Warren and Brown outside the public comfort station.

Espey was in fact a forty-five-year-old married man with a seven-year-old daughter. Born in Illinois in 1869, Espey lived with his parents in Los Angeles, where he worked as a butcher. He had run into previous trouble when he was charged with "embezzlement" while employed by a Mr. Newlee to run a butcher's wagon. He failed to turn in any money for twenty-four hours.

Espey paid the money back but came up with the story for his defense that "after he had been out a little while he got disgusted with life and put up the rig. Then he blew the proceeds of his sales in an endeavor to drown his sorrows in bad liquor." The

Plaintiff in Remarkable Libel Case.

C. E. Espey

Of Long Beach, who is suing the Times-Mirror Company for alleged libel, the action based upon publications made during the Long Beach vice clean-up.

Front-page coverage of Espey libel suit against the Times-Mirror Company. *From the* Los Angeles Daily Times, *October 27, 1916.*

charges were dismissed because there was no evidence of "criminal intent."

He moved to Long Beach and lived with his in-laws. Espey became very active in the Methodist Church. He became a real estate agent like his father-in-law and accumulated considerable wealth. His mother had an art studio in Los Angeles. His wife, Olive, was active in the Gaviota Chapter of the Daughters of the American Revolution.

Like the others arrested by the special officers, Espey initially pleaded guilty and paid a $500 fine. As the furor over Lamb's suicide increased, Espey hired Lowe's attorney, Roland Swaffield, to file for trial.

When Espey told the newspapers that he was innocent and had been blackmailed by Warren and Brown, Judge Hart ordered his arrest and charged him again with being a social vagrant.

While Espey waited for his day in court, the trial of Herbert Lowe began, again with a vigorous defense by Roland Swaffield.

Roland G. Swaffield was born in 1884 in Coldwater, Michigan, and moved to Long Beach in 1907 after graduating from law school at the University of Michigan. He married in 1907 and opened a solo law practice.

In 1910, he started a second law practice in Los Angeles with John G. Mulholland. Roland's brother Philip joined his Long Beach office, which became Swaffield & Swaffield.

Roland was extremely ambitious. In 1912, he ran as the Republican candidate for the Thirty-Third State Senate District, losing to the Democrat candidate.

The City of Long Beach periodically hired Swaffield to assist the city attorney in handling its cases. In 1914, he was retained for $2,400 to defend the city against $365,000 in damage claims filed by the families of the victims of the Empire Day pier collapse. He later resigned, citing that he had been "insulted and ignored" by the city council in how he wanted to handle the claims.

Because of Swaffield's connections with the City of Long Beach and his close personal friendship with its movers and shakers, he became the attorney to retain concerning legal matters involving the city, even criminal cases such as lewd vagrancy.

Swaffield was an aggressive litigator and defended his clients vigorously. His strategy for defending Reverend Franklin, Herbert Lowe and Charles Espey was the same: convince the jurors and the public at large that his clients were known residents and had been victims of a put-up job by outsiders.

Fisher wrote McClatchy:

Swaffield takes the attitude that "social vagrancy" is a disease rather than a crime and calls for special treatment. He declares that the majority of the cases in Long Beach involved the arrests of innocent men and declares that the result of this trail and publicity will be that in the future the vice crusaders will be dead sure they have the goods on an alleged social vagrant before effecting his arrest.

Special Officers Warren and Brown finally returned to Long Beach to testify against Herbert Lowe. As they took the stand, each laid out their sordid details of what led to the arrest of Lowe and the supposed information he offered about the conduct of the other men.

Brown explained that he targeted Lowe and stopped by his floral shop to talk. After Lowe took an interest in him, Brown asked to rent his cottage behind his home, which Brown referred to as a "love cottage." Brown told the jury that Chief of Police Cole had provided money for him to rent the cottage because of his suspicions concerning Lowe.

Three days after he moved into the cottage, Brown claimed that Lowe began visiting him in the early hours with surprise visits "at four o'clock in the morning."

Defendant Herbert Lowe (*left*) with his attorneys Roland and Phil Swaffield. *From the* Los Angeles Times. *November 19, 1914.*

Brown testified that one morning Lowe asked him if he cared to go surf bathing and offered to lend Brown a swimsuit. Brown then claimed that Lowe accompanied him to his rental to try on the swimsuit:

> *Lowe at first looked through the screen door as I was undressing and putting on the suit, but after I had nearly finished, he came in and helped me button it up, afterwards taking liberties. He patted me on the back and arms and said it fitted me just right.*

The next morning, according to Brown, Officer Remelt was positioned in the attic with his "eye to a peephole" chiseled through the wall and paper. He had slept the entire night in the attic.

> *He* [Lowe] *came in before I had awakened. Lowe pulled the clothes off of me and began the actions of the day before. I turned away and pulled up the clothes again. Lowe said: "I am sorry I can't stay longer, or we could have a good time."*

Ignoring that Officer Remelt could see that he had an erection, Brown dressed and set off for the public comfort station. He had work to do and bounties to earn.

Brown claimed that the next day Lowe exhibited the same behavior and told him of the secret clubs and their practices.

> *He asked me if I had ever heard of the Six-0-Six and the Ninety-Six Club. I said I had not. He said that the Ninety-Six Club was the best. That it was composed of the "queer" people, that got together every week. I asked Lowe why they called it the Ninety-Six Club and he said something about turning the letters around, before, and behind. He said that the members sometimes spent hundreds of dollars on silk gowns, hosiery, etc., in which they dressed at sessions of this club. He said that at these "drags" the "queer" people have a good time, but no one could get in without being introduced by a member in good standing. He offered to take me to the club at the next meeting.*

When Swaffield asked Brown what he was doing as Lowe was getting "familiar" and allegedly kissing his body and mouth, Brown responded:

> *I did not like it, and, moving a little farther away, kept on reading my magazine. Then Lowe came over to where I was and made the remark that*

I was getting fleshier or something like that. He pulled back the blankets. A minute later I heard a noise outside the window. Warren or his friend had accidentally betrayed their presence by slipping the gravel. Just then Warren and the officer rushed in to arrest Lowe.

Swaffield questioned Brown several times on the accuracy of his testimony, noting it had changed over the course of the first and second trial. Each time, either Brown or Warren strenuously argued that their testimony was correct and used the opportunity to add even more details about their interactions with Lowe.

Warren stated that when he arrested Lowe, he cried out, "What does this mean, Beal?" pleading with Brown. Brown explained to Lowe that he was being arrested because of the "queer things" he had done to him. Lowe then requested to be taken through the back streets saying that the publicity would "kill his father and mother," who lived in the front house with him.

Warren claimed that as they were riding to the police station, Lowe tried to bribe him with $1,000 and then broke down and revealed even more details of the secret clubs. Fisher confirmed to McClatchy that it was reported that Lowe offered "1,500" to be released.

Swaffield used the testimony to tell the jurors that Warren had told others that what he did was "easy money" because all he had to do was this:

Catch some fellows at the bath-house comfort station, take them around to the rear of the bathhouse and get all the money they had on them, in addition to all the checks he could get, and then tear up a blank check he took from his pocket and tell the fellow he was free and not to come back again.

Each and every day of the trial, Herbert Lowe's eighty-two-year-old father, Charles, sat in the courtroom, stoically listening to this testimony against his son. When the trial ended, Charles Lowe suffered a fatal heart attack at Herbert's home, reportedly from the stress of the trial and publicity.

Tempers flared inside and out of the courtroom as Swaffield disclosed to the judge and jury that Brown had made threats against him. In an attempt to expose Brown and Warren as "outsiders," Swaffield questioned Warren about his personal life and his lack of connections to Long Beach. Swaffield did not know that Warren was married and was stunned when Warren reached for his gun on his hip and fiercely challenged Swaffield to speak "respectfully about Mrs. Warren." This prompted Swaffield to request the judge to order Warren to put his handgun on the judge's desk so he could not shoot him during the trial.

Stirring up matters even more, the *Los Angeles Times* reported that death threats had been made against Judge Hart and the *Times'* Long Beach reporter. They printed a note sent to their reporter:

> *Correspondent C.C. Hurley: Your life will not be worth a picayune if you live in Long Beach another day. This committee of citizens will not stand for any more knocks on Long Beach. We have taken law into our own hands. Get out or be laid out. Signed Long Beach Vigilance Committee.*

The note was handed over to the detective bureau of Long Beach Police headed by Sergeant Fred Kutz. No one was ever charged.

Bathing suits worn in 1914. *Library of Congress.*

Swaffield used his closing remarks to remind jurors again of the suicide of John Lamb and the fact that Warren and Brown were not from Long Beach.

You don't know these stool pigeons who came here to "get" our citizens; you do know Lowe, who has been here for ten years. We don't need strangers to come here to ferret out crime.

Pointing to Warren in the courtroom, Swaffield said:

Look at the man who asks you to believe his testimony. See the puffs beneath the eyes, the sallow complexion, the sleek-combed and oil hair, the pink manicured fingernails. There is the degenerate. These men, Warren and Brown, are not to be believed by you. Their fingers are dripping with the blood of John Lamb. This was a frame up by "Special Officers" who were to get $10 a head for every man they arrested on the charge of being a lewd and dissolute person.

It took the jury less than thirty minutes to acquit Herbert Lowe on December 11, 1914. Attorney Swaffield had convinced the jury that the "outsider" special officers had conducted a put-up job. He was so persuasive that the jurors even ignored the testimonies of Chief of Police Cole and Detectives Mitchell and Cervantes, who stated Lowe had fully confessed to them.

Judge Hart was quick to point out that only once in three years had a Long Beach jury brought a conviction in his court. "Nineteen times out of twenty the jurors find some reason for acquitting the defendant."

In the following days, a grateful Herbert Lowe delivered floral arrangements to the jurors who acquitted him. Long Beach police told the newspapers that they were still pursuing members of the 606 Club

In sensational Long Beach trial.

Special Officers W.H. Warren (*left*) and B.C. Brown, hired by Mayor Whealton. *From the* Los Angeles Times, *November 19, 1914.*

Photograph of Harry Wharton of Long Beach, allegedly found by police when arresting a member of the never located "606 Club." *Correspondence file of C.K. McClatchy and Eugene I. Fisher, Center for Sacramento History.*

and had found a photograph in the home of Harry A. Wharton, who lived at 1911 East Tenth Street.

Fisher shared with McClatchy that photograph. He explained his police sources alleged they found the photograph in the possession of a man they arrested who was a member of the 606 Club. Fisher asked McClatchy for it to be returned so it could be published locally.

The photograph, which was published in the *Los Angeles Daily Times*, featured Wharton in woman's clothes outside his bungalow. Police claimed Wharton was a "prominent member of the club and boasted one of the finest wardrobes among the 'queer' people."

Long Beach was not finished with the issue of social vagrants. Charles Espey's trial proceeded, during which he denied the allegations. Espey explained that he, his wife and their eleven-year-old daughter had been visiting his wife's parents on Ocean Avenue for dinner. Later they went to the Pike to listen to a concert at the band shell, and Espey walked over to a "booth" near the bathhouse. When he emerged, he was confronted by Officer Warren, who placed him under arrest. Espey testified that he asked the nature of the charges and that Warren responded that he had been there "too long." Brown then informed him that he would find out at the station what he had done.

Espey testified that he pleaded guilty when taken to the police station because he knew they were blackmailers who asked him how much money he had on him when they arrested him.

During the trial, another prominent resident and bank president, Ira Hatch, testified that he had contacted Judge Hart on learning of Espey's arrest and was assured that if he gave a check in the amount of $500 for Espey's bail that the case would be at an end.

The jury deliberated nine hours, as one of the twelve jurors held out against acquittal because of the police testimony of the "special way" they marked social vagrants in public comfort stations. They testified that they had marked Espey and others with an indelible cross during his time in the public comfort station. Espey had admitted he was marked but argued that the ink had been "squirted" on him as he left the comfort station.

Charles Espey was acquitted by all twelve jurors. He requested that the court order his fine be overturned, but the court and city council rejected his request.

18

SACRAMENTO BEE AND LOS ANGELES TIMES TAUNT LONG BEACH OVER HOLY CITY IMAGE

The acquittal of Lowe and Espey and the failure to prosecute Reverend Baker infuriated *Sacramento Bee* publisher McClatchy. He lashed out at those who complained about the disclosure of these cases.

The *Bee* continued publishing articles concerning Reverend Baker, who had left California. McClatchy was obsessed and leveled accusations that were never proven. He railed against Baker escaping trial because of his connections. McClatchy claimed that acting police chief Samuel L. Browne told him that Lowe confessed to being a "degenerate":

The Case of Rev. Baker. In illustration of the statement that money and influence are on the side of the accused, of the known, confessed degenerate, I will cite the case of Rev. Franklin K. Baker, Unitarian Minister, once of Sacramento.

On October 9, 1913, Baker, at that time pastor of a Long Beach church, was arrested in a crowd in front of 326 South Main Street, Los Angeles. He had been under suspicion for some time and was shadowed for ten days by Detectives Shy and Burgess of the Los Angeles Police Department....

Why Some Escape. Those who carefully have read the preceding articles on the subjects to which The Bee is calling attention, will realize how easy it was in the case of Baker, and is in the care of prominent degerates [sic],

Long Beach.

POLICE GUARD AT THE DOOR.

Long Beach Officials Order an Open Trial.

Ban on Poison Sales Lifted by Chief Cole.

Ministers Avoid Reference to Notorious Scandal.

[LOCAL CORRESPONDENCE.]

THE HOLY CITY OF LONG BEACH, Nov. 15. — Chief of Police Cole has detailed a squad of policemen to stand guard in and about the courtroom when the trial of Herbert N. Lowe, wealthy florist and alleged "social vagrant," which is to be begun in Police Judge J. J. Hart's court tomorrow morning at 10 o'clock. It promises to be the most sensational trial ever held in this city. The details surrounding the apprehension of thirty-one men on the charge that they were "lewd persons" will not be censored. The trial will be public, the attorneys and court announced today.

Special Officers Warren and Brown will tell on the stand at the outset of their raids upon comfort stations on the beach, and upon certain cottages in this city, notably that of Lowe at Broadway and Junipero street. Chief Cole and four of his regular policemen will also be witnesses for the State. Attorneys Roland G. Swaffield and Phillip Swaffield will appear for Lowe. Deputy District Attorney Ong

Article mocking Long Beach as "The Holy City." *From the* Los Angeles Times, *November 16, 1914.*

to slip out of the clutches of the law. The newspapers gave little space to the Baker case. The public took little interest in it. The story was a very minor sensation for a day, one episode among thousands. Men are awakening [sic] to the enormity of these offenses against nature of which members of the "96," "606," and other clubs are guilty.

The *Los Angeles Times* also published articles taunting Long Beach as a "holy city."

Fisher reminded McClatchy that the crimes committed in Long Beach were prosecuted only as misdemeanors and that he needed to use his friends in the state legislature to pass a bill that would make oral sex punishable as a felony:

There is no law under which this crime against nature is punishable directly, hence they are arrested and prosecuted as "social vagrants" and lewd and dissolute persons. These creatures are now operating in and around Los Angeles, San Francisco, Chicago, and other great American and European cities and are not even satisfied with this unnatural and degrading practice. Their passion and desire still is for young boys and girls but they take their pleasure in the still more loathsome and disgusting way of applying their mouths to the private parts of their companions in crime in what they are pleased to call the "Twentieth Century Way."

McClatchy took up the campaign to change the sodomy law in California and wrote:

It should be remembered that social vagrants are not indigenous to Southern California. The South's efforts to run down a few, at least, of the degenerates within her borders has centered attention upon herself. But degeneracy is in Sacramento, San Francisco and every city, town and hamlet in the Nation. It grows as population increases and as luxury and idleness become more general.

Press Can Supply Lever. With these forces as a fulcrum the press can supply the lever that will overturn a vicious system that is striking deep at the root of social welfare in all parts of the country.

Yes the California law classes it as a comparatively trifling matter, a mere misdemeanor, punishable by a small fine, a short time in jail. Or fine and jail, if the Court is particularly lenient.

The editor of the *Bryon Times* praised the *Sacramento Bee* for publishing the details of the Long Beach scandal and penned an editorial on January 1, 1915, calling to "Make It a Felony":

> *More power to the* Bee. *And let it be hoped that other newspapers will take hold of this matter, disagreable* [sic] *though it be, and keep at it until a law is passed that moral lepers who infest a commnity* [sic] *shall be made to suffer for their unspeakable crime, than which no greater disgrace can be found upon the face of the earth.*

In 1915, California became the first state to outlaw "cunnilingus and fellatio" by expanding its sodomy law. Section 288a of the California Penal Code provided,

> *The acts technically known as fellatio and cunnilingus are hereby declared to be felonies and any person convicted of the commission of thereof shall be punished by imprisonment in the state prison for not more than fifteen years.*

A year later, in the case of *People v. Carell*, the appellate court ruled that the words *cunnilingus* and *fellatio* were not English words:

> *An indictment or information must contain a statement of acts constituting the offense in ordinary and concise language, and in such manner as to enable a person of common understanding to know what is intended….Unexplained, the word "fellatio" would, to a man of common understanding (indeed, we think also to one of uncommon understanding), be as cabalistic as if written in Egyptian or Mexican hieroglyphics or in Japanese or Chinese characters.*

Several similar cases came before the courts on the same issue—that the words in the penal code were not English. In 1918, the California Supreme Court ruled that the word *fellatio* could be found in most medical dictionaries and upheld the law. One year later, the court reversed itself in the case, "In re Application of Clarence Lockett for a Writ of Habeas Corpus," and ruled that the penal code inclusion of "fellatio and cunnilingus" made the code "void for vagueness" and therefore unconstitutional. The state legislature passed a new law using the words *oral copulation* to make clear to the public what acts were illegal.

19

WHEALTON FIGHTS NEW FORM OF CITY GOVERNMENT

Mayor Louis Whealton did not like the outcome of the city election, in which voters approved a new charter and a new form of government. The new charter shortened his current term of office by six months.

While the newspapers focused on the Lowe trial, Whealton mounted a campaign to overturn the charter vote by urging residents to sign a petition that would forbid City Clerk Harry Riley from submitting the new charter to the state legislature for ratification.

When the petition failed, Whealton and Scott Alexander filed a request for a restraining order from the Superior Court to prevent the city clerk from delivering the approved charter to the state legislature.

Whealton sensed there might be some weakness in the support of the new charter, as out of the large electorate, only 3,274 people voted, 1,651 in favor and 1,605 opposed. Scott Alexander, owner of the Hotel Alexander, tried to help Whealton overturn the new charter because of his opposition to the changes made in liquor rights in hotels and apartments.

Thinking that City Clerk Riley had the only official copy of the newly written charter, Whealton "kidnapped" it from the city clerk's office, only to discover there were four copies. One had been filed with the county recorder, and the city clerk had boarded a train to Sacramento with the two other official copies.

Hotel Alexander on First Street in downtown Long Beach, next to the bank Lamb served as member of the board of directors. *Author's collection.*

Whealton and Alexander told the court that the copies taken to Sacramento by Clerk Riley contained "more than seventy" spelling and grammatical errors, and had voters thirty-four thousand words with "inconsequential typographical errors" and denied the request for the restraining order.

After Riley took the two copies of the new charter to Sacramento, Whealton then contacted Assemblyman Joseph Rominger and asked that he contact the state attorney general for an opinion on two provisions of the new charter. First, could street improvements be authorized by a commission instead of the city council and second, could the charter be amended in less than the two years allowed?

The new charter was accepted by the state legislature and sent to both the governor and the secretary of state.

Whealton wrote numerous articles for the local newspapers denying that his opposition to the new charter had anything to do with the fact his term of office was being shortened. He also denied any interest in serving as the commissioner of the fire and police departments, which some of his supporters urged him to accept should he not seek reelection.

Samuel Browne sued the City of Long Beach for backpay promised by Whealton. The city council refused to pay the $644 owed, stating that it was Whealton and not the city council who hired Browne.

Before he left office, Whealton tried to push for the city to establish a natural gas distribution system by putting up $300,000 to purchase the Fullerton Gas Fields. He vowed that after his term expired, he would take up the fight with funds raised by Scott Alexander and other wealthy citizens.

Unveiling of Lincoln statue placed in Pacific Park in 1915 just days before Mayor Whealton left office. *Library of Congress.*

Even though his term as mayor was ending in July 1915, Whealton managed to take over the July 3 dedication of the statue of Abraham Lincoln placed in the City's Pacific Park. The statue was a monument to the men of the Great Army of the Republic who served in the Civil War. The streets and park were jammed with residents and visitors who also came to see USS *Chattanooga* offshore. A program was printed that included a full-page photograph of Louis N. Whealton, mayor of Long Beach.

20

ARRESTEE SUES FOR BEING SLANDERED DURING STORIES ON LONG BEACH

Almost a year to the day the newspaper article that drove John Lamb to suicide appeared, Charles Espey retained the legal firm of Swaffield and Swaffield to sue the Times-Mirror Company for publishing in the *Los Angeles Times* on November 14, 1914, an article that included his name as a "social vagrant." Espey sued for libel and asked for $100,000 in damages.

It took two years for his case to come to trial, during which the *Los Angeles Times* published detailed accounts of what Espey allegedly did to be arrested and how the special officers obtained evidence of his crime. The details had never been published before, so in essence, Espey was retried in public. The disclosure also implicated what John Lamb had been accused of doing in the public comfort station.

The matter of the indelible marking on Espey and the other men arrested in the public comfort station was described in great detail during the libel trial. Brown's deposition laid out that he and Warren had witnessed Espey commit "unnatural acts" in the comfort station and "placed a tell-tale mark on him" before they took him to the police station. Brown could not describe how it actually was placed on Espey.

Brown's testimony could not be supported by Warren because he failed to appear at the Espey trial. William "Billy" Warren had paid a young man ten dollars to buy a gun, which he used to murder his woman-friend Creta Carter. He then turned the gun on himself and shot his heart twice.

A photograph was placed in evidence showing the comfort station toilet with a hole in the partition between it and another toilet.

Long Beach Police booking sergeant Llewellyn testified that he saw a one-inch-long mark on Espey when he processed him.

Ex-mayor Whealton testified he employed Detectives Warren and Brown to "expose and punish degenerates who infested Long Beach in 1914," even though there was little evidence supporting his claim.

The Times-Mirror attorney, George P. Adams, told the jury that the *Los Angeles Times* published Espey's name only once, that his name was verified from court records as having pleaded guilty and that the newspaper never said he was guilty or a member of the secret clubs.

Adams also pointed out that during the trial, Espey never once flinched at the disclosure of the crime he was accused of committing:

> *Mr. Espey comes up here, says he is innocent, sits here and listens to all of this array of despicable, low, contemptible, rotten stuff about him and never a blush mantles his cheek. Why, you gentlemen, have blushed at some of the evidence here, and so has everybody but Mr. Espey. With Mr. Espey it is a business proposition. If one of you gentlemen were charged with the commission of a crime one-tenth as loathsome and debasing as this charge that was made against Mr. Espey and someone sat here on the witness stand and testified about that, you would hang your heads in shame. What about Mr. Espey? He sat up here and never quiver. You could not have picked out in the courtroom the man who was charged with those things from anything that appeared on Mr. Espey's countenance.*

Judge Monroe instructed the jury:

> *Proprietors of newspapers are not to be punished for publishing a fair, full, and true report of a judicial proceeding except upon actual proof of malice in making the report, and they also have the right to make just, fair, and responsible comments upon a deduction from facts disclosed in judicial proceedings. If you find that the sting of the charged is true, then your verdict should be for the defendant.*

The jury found in favor of Times-Mirror Company, and Espey recovered nothing.

America went to war, and Long Beach turned its attention to other things. It did, however, continue to embrace the theater of female impersonators.

Photographs revealing Julian Eltinge as a male and female impersonator. *Library of Congress.*

In 1919, famed female impersonator Julian Eltinge came to Long Beach to give two sold-out performances at the Hoyt Theater on the Pike. Reviewers noted that Eltinge was bringing "his original sketch, his repertoire of songs and his stunning gowns." Audiences were filled with women, who fought for standing room. They claimed to appreciate Eltinge because he knew what it took to be a woman.

Eltinge devised *The Ten Mysteries of Woman*, which he divulged in newspaper interviews was performed to explain what he had uncovered during his many years' study of female psychology, deportment, manners and "blandishments." Women followers often commented that Eltinge understood women better than any other man.

Female and male impersonators continued to perform in Long Beach theaters, at church fundraisers and on the movie screen. Eltinge left the stage and appeared in movies such as *The Countess Charming* and *The Widow's Might*, a comedy written by Marion Fairfax and directed by William C. deMille.

21

THE FINAL TRIAL ON 1914 SCANDAL

L ong Beach was to read one more time about the 1914 scandal and the suicide of John A. Lamb.

Los Angeles Tribune publisher and editor E.T. Earl filed a lawsuit against Times-Mirror for libelous comments in their articles referring to him and his newspapers as defending "degenerates" and "sodomites" in the Long Beach scandal.

Earl reminded readers of his history in the "fruit-shipping business" and how he invented a combined ventilator and refrigerator car and operated a "refrigerator car line for many years." His success allowed him to purchase the *Los Angeles Evening Press* in 1901 and start the *Los Angeles Morning Tribune* in 1911 as "the first 1-cent morning paper in California."

Earl argued through his attorneys that the *Los Angeles Times* articles were part of an ongoing attack by the publisher and that the jurymen should put themselves in his place if they were called "defenders of degenerates and sodomites."

EDWIN T. EARL
Publisher of Evening Express and Morning Tribune

Edwin T. Earl, publisher of *Evening Express* and *Morning Tribune*, featured himself in articles about his libel suit against *Times-Mirror*. *From the* Evening Express, *November 28, 1916.*

On November 27, 1916, "after four hours and nine minutes of deliberation," the jury found for Earl.

Earl filled the pages of the *Los Angeles Express* with details and commentary on the trial. After the ruling, he wrote:

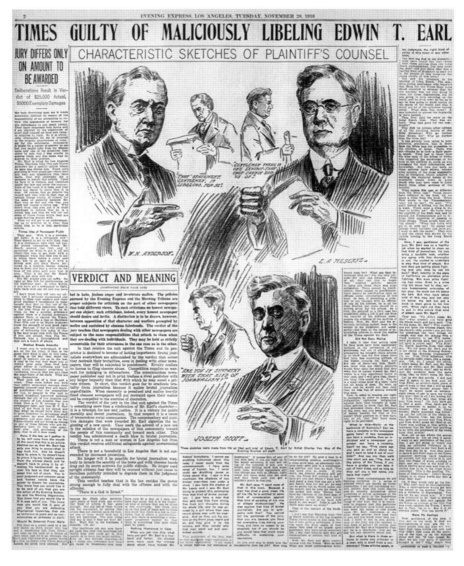

When Earl won, he published several articles detailing the trial. *From the* Evening Express, *November 28, 1916.*

The verdict of the jury tells its own story. It is the answer justice makes to wrongdoing. It interprets the judgment not only of the law, but of society. It is responsive to the direct appeal, that, in its findings, the jury, casting all personal prejudice and personal feelings aside, should, by its verdict, discharge a duty to honest men and honest women everywhere, who are made to suffer under the lash of brutal journalism. The verdict is at once an example and a warning—an example to other juries here or elsewhere that may be called upon to determine like cases, a warning to offenders that the laws of this land will not permit the powers of publicity to be used in destructive malice.

This case is destined to establish a precedent of abiding value. Its lessons reach alike to the victims and to the practitioners of brutal journalism. From this verdict the innocent sufferers from that sort of journalism will learn that retribution can be exacted and by this lesson journalists who lend themselves to brutal practices will be taught that before a just judge and a just jury they cannot hope to escape punishment for these offenses.

Times-Mirror appealed the damages award, arguing not all jurors were in favor of the total. Earl died in 1919, and his heirs had to wait until February 25, 1921, when the California Supreme Court affirmed the lower court decisions that:

charging the publisher of a rival newspaper with being the defender of degenerates for hire reprehensible that it must necessarily affect his standing the community and expose him to obloquy and contempt.

The Supreme Court upheld the verdict of $25,000 compensatory damages but denied the additional $5,000 against all defendants.

After the coverage of the libel suits, there was no more mention of the 1914 arrests in local newspapers until 2016, when a Superior Court judge noted in his decision that Long Beach was still singling out gay men in public restrooms.

22

LONG BEACH CONTINUES TARGETING GAY MEN IN PUBLIC RESTROOMS UNTIL 2016

T he events surrounding the arrest and suicide of John A. Lamb are featured in several academic journals, books and a short play titled *The Twentieth Century Way* by Tom Jacobson.

Several of these sources contain incorrect facts, such as the number or ages of those arrested or the fact that the existence of the secret societies was never corroborated. None discuss the full contents of Lamb's suicide note in which he named his close friend and a prominent real estate agent as being possibly behind his arrest. None mention the links between the political motivations or professional connections of the major characters that drove this scandal.

We need to learn from history. Homosexuality or "lewd vagrants" were not a problem for the voters in Long Beach in 1914, neither was the issue of men impersonating women. Politicians and newspaper publishers chose to exploit men who sought the company of other men. It should be noted again that most of the men arrested who paid their fines were upper class and well-off. The ones who could not afford the high fees had to serve time in the local jails.

This book specifically highlights the danger of popular politicians and news outlets that exploit marginalized groups for political purposes. It is important to know what happened to several of the key characters in order to get a sense of how the events affected their lives.

It is also critical to know that the singling out of gay men in public restrooms for arrest did not stop in Long Beach until 2016, when the court ruled that the targeting of men in public restrooms in Long Beach was "discriminatory."

The story of how the political leaders used gay men as political fodder in Long Beach in 1914 and continued to target them is not to discount the facts that since then, Long Beach, California, has become a much more progressive city.

Long Beach, like other cities, has a lengthy history of using police force against gay men while often ignoring other "lewd" conduct.

Long Beach City Council passed an ordinance in 1955 banning the possession of "lewd photographs" and made many arrests. The police also focused on "lewd shows" held in places like the clubhouse of the Veterans of Foreign Wars. These shows, however, featured naked women, and although the newspaper reported there had been more than "200 in attendance," not one person was arrested or publicly named. Police told the newspaper that they were checking to find the man who rented the building and they "might make an arrest later."

D. Patrick Ahern was elected to Long Beach City Council in the late 1950s and focused on urging the Long Beach Police Department to "rid Long Beach of seven homosexual hangouts." He campaigned for U.S. Congress on the platform that he helped Long Beach police "rid" the city of five bars. He lost his election.

In 1951, the California Supreme Court ruled the Black Cat Restaurant in San Francisco could not lose its liquor license for serving homosexuals. After the ruling, gay bars flourished but police raids continued. The gay community began fighting back. In 1968, patrons of the Patch in Wilmington, owned by Long Beach resident Lee Glaze, staged a protest at the Harbor Police Station after two patrons were arrested. As the police took them away, Glaze jumped on stage, yelling, "It's not against the law to be a homosexual, and it's not a crime to be in a gay bar!" Glaze rallied his customers to chant, "We're Americans too!" Protestors bought all of the flowers at a local florist and took them to the police station at 3:00 a.m. The police did not know how to respond to the "flower power protest" and released the two.

In 1953, a group of men gathered in east Long Beach to discuss forming the Long Beach Area Council of the Mattachine Society no. 113. Mattachine was an organization started in Los Angeles by Henry Hay to "protect and improve the rights of gay men." The name was taken from a medieval group of men who went about the countryside entertaining and wearing colorful masques and remaining anonymous. According to the U.S. Library of Congress:

The patrons of the Patch in Wilmington protested the arrest of two men by bringing flowers to the police station. *From* Q Voice News.

The Mattachine Society (initially called the Mattachine Foundation) began as a secret organization in Los Angeles in 1950, with their first Statement of Purpose drawn up in 1951. The group was founded by Communist organizer Harry Hay and other leftists including Bob Hull, Chuck Rowland, Dale Jennings, Konrad Stevens, James Gruber and Rudi Gernreich (Jewish Refugee). The Mattachine founders borrowed the initial structure of the organization from the Communist Party, and the leadership, the "fifth order" was anonymous, so members didn't even know their names. The Mattachine Society went on to become one of several prominent groups organizing during the period of LGBTQ+ activism referred to as the Homophile Movement, with chapters opening up in a number of states.

In 1961, the U.S. Navy made an official complaint with the City of Long Beach concerning the "menace to Navy personnel in the area from civilian homosexuals." The police and the shore patrol agreed to step up enforcement against this activity. Interestingly, Long Beach had been home to the U.S. Navy since before World War II and was known as a welcoming place for homosexual sailors.

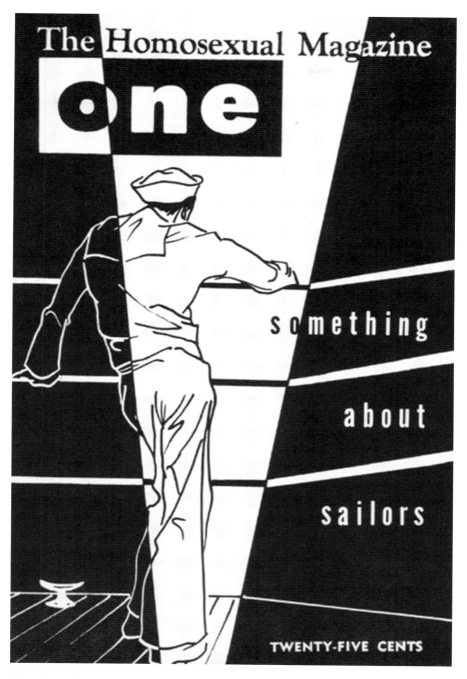

Since the early 1900s, Long Beach has been a home port for the U.S. Navy. Many sailors patronized the local gay bars. *ONE Archives at the USC Libraries*.

Calls were made to step up military patrols and local police enforcement of public restrooms and gay bars so that Long Beach could rid itself of the name "Paradise for Pansies."

On August 18, 1966, the issue of local homosexuals "preying on" young sailors was the subject of a lengthy column in the *Independent Press Telegram* by columnist George Robeson. He falsely claimed that homosexuals were pedophiles and never discussed the possibility that the sailors were homosexual. He wrote:

> *South End Is Home for Homosexuals.*
> *CAN YOU GUESS what your city was called recently, Citizen? "A Paradise for Pansies." That's what it was called. Normally, I would ignore this, because the name-caller was a cheap national tabloid that sells the most lurid details of sex and blood, written by reporters who make it up as they go along. But this time, the tabloid spoke the truth. The homosexual problem in Long Beach is a big one because its principal victims are young sailors. It is evil because of the strategy of recruitment. Patrolmen, attorneys, and judges would tell you that the majority of the homosexuals preying on young servicemen here come from Hollywood or Los Angeles. They come here, to a port city, a Navy town, because the pickings are better. Police would tell you that most weekends result in at least 10 arrests of homosexuals. They will tell you that for each of those arrests, there are innumerable pickups made by homosexuals. Being observed by police.*
>
> *TO A HOMOSEXUAL in Long Beach the ideal victim is a teen-ager or young serviceman. The target areas are the public restrooms on the beach, from the Nu-Pike to Belmont Shore, or those at Lincoln Park; the street-corners along First Street on Broadway and Ocean Boulevard and their intersections with Long Beach Boulevard; and the Greyhound Bus Station.*

Robeson's attacks faded out as the navy began leaving Long Beach.

In 1969, employees, patrons, and neighbors of the Stonewall Inn in Greenwich Village, New York, protested against the constant arrest, shakedown and harassment of gay patrons. The bar was owned by a Mafia family and provided watered-down drinks and poorly maintained premises. But it also provided a place where gays and lesbians could meet and dance. Homosexual contact was a crime at the time, and while on most occasions the bar owners were tipped off by the police, they paid for protection so that when police arrived, the bar appeared "normal."

On a hot summer day in 1969, the bar owners were not tipped off and police raided the bar, beating some with nightsticks and arresting everyone inside. Hundreds took to the street, forcing the police to barricade themselves inside the bar. The gay community had had enough, and the nation took notice.

Throughout the country, gay and lesbians formed organizations in their communities.

In Long Beach in 1971, the International Imperial Court of Long Beach Inc. (IICLB, also known as the Long Beach Imperial Court) began. It is the longest-running LGBTQ nonprofit in the greater Long Beach Metro area. With a mission to give back to the community by raising funds for other LGBTQ nonprofits through innovative fundraisers, initiatives and advocacy, the IICLB has become one of the most effective fundraising forces in Long Beach. Since its founding, the IICLB has raised over $1 million for local community causes. The IICLB is one of nearly seventy chapters of the International Imperial Court System that spans three countries: the United States of America, Canada and Mexico. Every chapter in the Imperial Court System is led by an empress, an emperor or an emprex. Each reign is typically led by two monarchs. Elected by

The Imperial Court is the oldest LGBTQ nonprofit in Long Beach. *JustinRudd.com.*

EXPERIENCE OUR TOTALLY NEW ATMOSPHERE

Que Sera Sera

MELISSA
WED. 8-11 P.M., NO COVER
FRI. 7-10 P.M., $2 COVER
AFTER 7 P.M.

THE SECRETARIES
SUNDAY NIGHT
$2 COVER

MON.-FRI. 3 P.M.-2 A.M.
SAT.-SUN. 2 P.M.-2 A.M.

HAPPY HOUR
MON.-FRI., 3 P.M.-7 P.M.
NO COVER SAT. NIGHT

1923 E. 7TH ST., LONG BEACH. 213/599-6170

Lesbian bar Que Sera, Sera was owned by Ellen Ward and featured musicians such as Melissa Etheridge. *Historical Society of Long Beach.*

members of the communities they serve, these individuals play a critical role in the organization and serve as the fundraising chairs for the upcoming year.

In 1973, the *Long Beach Independent Press Telegram* launched a three-part series on "the lesbian adjustment to homosexuality," explaining to readers how lesbians were in many ways like other women.

In 1975, Ellen Ward opened the lesbian bar Que Sera Sera and later helped launch the career of the young guitarist and singer Melissa Etheridge, who lived in Long Beach.

There were few bars for lesbians in Long Beach. To provide a place where women could meet, Carol Irene and Maria Dominquez, who were partners, opened up Long Beach's first and only "woman-identified" bookstore, Sojourner, on Redondo Avenue near Seventh Street in 1974. The store sold children's and adult books and magazines and offered a meeting room with a community bulletin board and hot water for coffee or tea.

The Gay Student Union at Long Beach State University organized and held the first Gay Pride Week and Gay-Think Conference in Long Beach in October 1975. The event drew prominent gay and lesbian performers and speakers such as Pat Harris and Robin Tyler, lesbian comedians, Rita Mae Brown and author Jean Cordova, publisher of the *Lesbian Tide*. Topics discussed included "gay liberation in the church, sexism in the gay movement, gay stereotypes in the media, blacks in the gay community, gay health care, sociology and gays, gays and the legal process, gay legal counseling, opening academic closets and Gay Pride National Celebration '76."

Long Beach police continued to arrest gay men in public restrooms and, this time, it was the local feminists who called out police for their "selective enforcement" in 1976. The feminists pointed out that the police "sex crimes unit" spent more time in the public restrooms arresting men than they did pursuing rapists and others who committed sexual assault against women. The feminists surmised that it took less effort to walk into a restroom and engage another man in what would be called illegal conduct than it would be to investigate and find rapists.

The number of public restroom arrests for "lewd conduct" was so high in 1976 that the Gay Student Union at California State University at Long Beach set up patrols of beach public restrooms in an attempt to stop the gay activity.

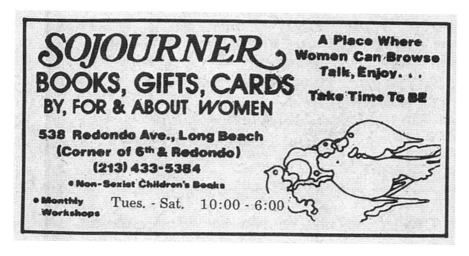

Sojourner Bookstore was an oasis for women in the 1970s. *Author's collection.*

On July 29, 1977, the *Press-Telegram* ran a story titled "Homosexuality Rife at Beaches and Parks" and warned readers:

> *Any parent who allows his child to go into a beach or park rest room unescorted in this city is either naive or doesn't care about his kid. A Long Beach Police Vice Police Sergeant has said in a warning about homosexual activity in recreation areas. Sgt. Jim Furman said parents should be aware of lewd conduct that occurs at all hours in recreation rest rooms, adding that anyone—including children—who uses these facilities runs the risk of viewing such acts.*

The reporter explained:

> *[The] notorious homosexual rendezvous—the restroom at the foot of Granada Avenue in Belmont Shore had been closed by the city causing homosexual activity at the rest rooms serving the Belmont Plaza Olympic pool area.*

He also pointed out that male homosexuals "sometimes use the women's side of the rest room for sexual contacts in an effort to elude police officers."

The article then casually mentioned an eight-year-old boy being raped in one of the Belmont Plaza restrooms:

> *Vice Capt. Bob Alford said child molestation was not the primary fear of vice officers who patrol these areas. The exposure of children to homosexual acts is. A child is more in danger of witnessing a lewd act than of being molested. I don't think we have a lot of child molesters running around.*

In the same edition, a small classified ad about "Militant Homosexuals" added to the scare tactics.

After the story ran, a man identifying himself as gay called the newspaper "Ombudsman" F.C. Anderson and complained that the story was fabricated by the police to keep people out of the public restroom. Anderson investigated and found that the story indeed had been made up.

By 1977, local press estimated the number of gay bars at forty. A Gay Bar Guild was formed to work with the Long Beach Department to "open a channel of communication."

The same year, the Long Beach Lambda Democratic Club started with its announced purposes:

Lambda Democratic Club was a political catalyst starting in the 1970s. A contingency of members marched in the annual Pride Parade. *Author's collection*.

Registration of sympathetic voters, monitoring the Long Beach Police Department and supporting the enactment of an employment act to forbid employers from discriminating against homosexuals.

In response to the national Save Our Children campaign led by orange juice commercial spokesperson Anita Bryant in opposition to gays and lesbians, a Long Beach chapter of Parents and Friends of Lesbians and Gays (PFLAG) was formed to provide support in 1977.

That same year, Lambda Democratic Club called a public meeting at a local bank with the Long Beach Police chief, Carl Calkins, and City Manager John Dever to protest the filing of a false report by police after a raid on the bar Brave Bull. The police chief publicly admitted that a false report had been filed and that he had suspended "four vice detectives." The chief also announced the reorganization of the vice unit, restricting assignment to only twenty-four months instead of permanently. He conceded that the police "sometimes get carried away and will try to impose certain moral values on other people."

As the gay and lesbian community became more active and visible, it started ONE In Long Beach in 1977 to help members of the community. In 1981, it opened the Unified Community Service Center at Tenth Street and Cherry Avenue.

ONE Incorporated formed in Los Angeles in 1952 as a "non-political, non-sectarian organization concerned with the interests of the millions of homosexual American men and women." It offered the ONE Institute of Homophile Studies, providing courses at undergraduate and graduate levels in world cultures, religion, law, morals, psychology, medicine and the arts. The courses give parents, ministers, doctors, lawyers, psychologists, sociologists and the general public an understanding of homosexuality and homosexuals to provide specialized training for those planning to work directly in this field. "Special emphasis was laid on sane personal adjustments for the homophile and the removal of guilt feelings and condemnation."

The State Proposition 6 was launched by State Senator John Briggs and put before the voters in 1978:

> [To] *allow the filing of criminal charges against schoolteachers, counselors, teachers' aides, administrators for advocating, soliciting, imposing, encouraging, or promoting private or public sexual acts designed in sections 286(a) and 288a(a) of the Penal Code between persons of same sex in a manner likely to come to the attention of other employees or students, or publicly and indiscreetly engaging in said acts. Prohibits hiring and requires dismissal of such persons if school board determines them unfit for service after considering enumerated guidelines. In dismissal cases only, provides for two-stage hearings, written findings, judicial review.*

The measure mobilized the LGBTQ+ community and its allies. The ballot measure was defeated on November 7, 1978, by 58.43 percent of the vote.

Just three weeks after the anti-gay measure was soundly defeated statewide, San Francisco mayor George Moscone and openly gay supervisor Harvey Milk were shot and killed by Dan White, another supervisor who was a former fireman and police officer. White had been elected in 1977 on a promise to "eradicate malignancies that blight our city." He was the only supervisor to vote against the San Francisco nondiscrimination ordinance. He also opposed permits for LGBTQ+ events and was quoted as saying,

NEWS
the center

. 1/NO. 12 • UNIFIED COMMUNITY SERVICE CENTER, 2017 EAST 4th STREET, LONG BEACH, CA 90804 • S

We've Moved ! ! !

FROM:
2025 E. 10th St.
Long Beach

TO:
2017 East
4th Street
Long Beach

. and we have a thirty-five
space parking lot behind
for your convenience

HOMECOMING
AT THE NEW CENTER!
FRIDAY, SEPTEMBER 19, 1986
6:00 p.m. — to 12 Midnight

Originally ONE in Long Beach, the organization eventually grew and established the United Community Service Center and today is known as the LGBTQ Center Long Beach. *LGBTQ Center Long Beach.*

"The vast majority of people in this city don't want public displays of sexuality."

White resigned from his position in the fall of 1978, claiming the pay was too low. He then immediately asked for his position back. When Mayor Moscone would not let him retract his resignation, White shot and killed him. White also killed Milk because he suspected Milk had supported Moscone in not allowing White to return to office. White was tried and convicted of voluntary manslaughter even though he confessed that he had premeditated the murders. He served eight years and killed himself on his release.

The Gay Pride Parade was a controversial issue in Long Beach. A Gay Pride Week patterned after one in West Hollywood was started in Long Beach, even though the organizers faced opposition from many in the gay community who did not believe the community should be so visible and violent threats from others.

Community activists formed the Lesbian and Gay Pride Inc. in 1983, headed by Marilyn Barlow, Bob Crow and Judi Doyle. LGP applied to the Long Beach City Council for a "gay pride parade permit" that would permit a festival and parade in celebration of the Stonewall protests. The city informed the group that it would need to pay approximately $31,000 in

Marilyn Barlow, Bob Crow and Judi Doyle formed the Long Beach Lesbian & Gay Pride Inc., which hosted the first Pride Parade and Festival in 1984. *Long Beach Pride.*

costs and obtain a $1 million insurance policy for the festival and parade. LGP Inc. reported that three hundred people attended the parade.

When the group applied for the same permit in 1985, it was again confronted with what it considered excessive fees. The National Association of Gay Pride Coordinators informed the Long Beach group that Long Beach was the only city of the thirteen that held parades to charge for police services and liability insurance.

LGP Inc. sued the City of Long Beach in 1985 and explained to the court:

> *The parade commemorates the lesbian and gay rights movement, publicly espouses such rights, and celebrates the participants' pride in their orientation while allowing them to enlighten the community about it. LBLGP has conducted the parade annually since 1984, on Sunday afternoons in May or June, along a 1.6-mile stretch of Ocean Boulevard, a main thoroughfare of the city. The parade includes both pedestrians and motor vehicles, some pulling floats; between 1984 and 1989 the approximate number of participants grew from 300 to 1000.*

It took until 1993 for the court to rule that the city had been arbitrary in its requirements for permits and liability insurance.

In 1982, a Republican state senator launched an investigation against a part-time instructor in the women's studies department at California State University at Long Beach. The senator alleged that the instructor had been advocating "lesbianism in the classroom" during her class titled "Women and Their Bodies."

Betty Brooks, a physical education instructor, admitted she had shown slides of her own genitals as a way to teach the students about their own bodies. The university fired Brooks, only to be sued by the American Civil Liberties Union. Brooks was reinstated. Brooks was a feminist activist in anti-rape work, women's sexuality and feminist theology. She was co-founder of the Rape Crisis Hotline and Women Against Sexual Abuse the Califia Community. After Brooks was reinstated, several members of the "religious right" continued attacking the women's studies department and the classes taught. This resulted in the American Civil Liberties Union filing what has been described as "the most significant academic freedom suit in two decades." It won.

The LGBT Center established Project Ahead in 1984 to help those affected by HIV and AIDS when few resources were offered by the city or local hospitals.

The local newspaper proclaimed by 1985 that Long Beach was the home to thirty-five to fifty thousand gays and lesbians. Parts of the city attracted gays and lesbians who purchased properties, turning some streets into what the *Los Angeles Times* termed a "gay mecca."

In 1986, a permanent LGBT Center was purchased, and it still operates on Fourth Street in Long Beach. The purchase was made possible by donations from the estates of those who passed away because of HIV and AIDS.

Subsequently, one lesbian and two openly gay men have been elected to public office in Long Beach. Another openly gay man, Richard Gaylord, ran unsuccessfully for city council in 1982 and for Long Beach Community College District Board of Trustees in 2020.

In 1992, the author, Gerrie Schipske, was elected to the Long Beach Community College District Board of Trustees and served as president during her tenure.

In 1999, Dan Baker was elected to city council and reelected. He ran for mayor unsuccessfully in 2002 and resigned from the city council in 2006 after being accused of an ethics violation of which he was later cleared.

In 2006 and 2010, Gerrie Schipske was elected to the Long Beach City Council.

Robert Garcia was elected to Long Beach City Council in 2009 and as mayor in 2014 and reelected in 2018.

In 1993, the city council voted unanimously to censure one of its members, who also was a retired Long Beach police commander, after a tape recording was disclosed with his remarks to a Long Beach chapter of the conservative Eagle Forum. He told the crowd that he was not worried about gays and lesbians in Long Beach because "they are dying of AIDS and do not reproduce." He was also heard saying he supported "Cuba's policy of quarantining people with deadly diseases" and termed allowing gays and lesbians to adopt as "pitiful."

The city council debated legalizing domestic partner status for city employees and residents in 1996. The city made national news when one of the councilmembers who was also a Los Angeles County deputy sheriff told a crowd at the council meeting that he was opposed to approving "domestic partnership rights for homosexuals" because:

> *The human sex drive is a powerful instinct that may become inappropriately affixed to underwear, corpses, animals, children, footstools, and members of the same sex. "What do we say to the man who leads his favorite ewe*

down the aisle, demanding recognition and acceptances of his attraction to a female sheep?"

The city council eventually approved a domestic partner registry in 1997 with the help of local activist Connie Hamilton.

During the 1996 primary for the Democratic nomination for an assembly seat, Gerrie Schipske was attacked by her African American opponent, who sent a mailer to voters warning that "Schipske has a gay agenda." Schipske won the nomination with over 60 percent and went on to lose the general election against a Republican incumbent by only 982 votes.

Since 2011, when the Municipal Equality Index Scorecard on LGBTQ+ issues was first developed by the Human Rights Campaign, Long Beach has received the highest rating. The Human Rights Campaign is a national organization based in Washington, D.C., that "strives to end discrimination against LGBTQ+ people and realize a world that achieves fundamental fairness and equality for all."

The Municipal Equality Index was designed by the HRC Foundation to help residents learn how inclusive their city's laws and policies are of LGBTQ+ people. Cities are rated on:

> *"Non-Discrimination" and evaluates whether discrimination on the basis of sexual orientation and gender identity is prohibited by the city in areas of employment, housing, and public accommodations.*

> *"Municipality as an Employer" and evaluates whether discrimination on the basis of sexual orientation and gender identity is prohibited by the city in areas of employment, housing, and public accommodations.*

> *"Municipal Services" and evaluates whether discrimination on the basis of sexual orientation and gender identity is prohibited by the city in areas of employment, housing, and public accommodations. It requires the Mayor's Office to employ an LGTQ+ Liaison to receive a perfect rating.*

> *"Law Enforcement" and requires responsible reporting of hate crimes and engaging with the LGBTQ+ community in a thoughtful and respectful way with employment of a LGBTQ+ liaison in the department.*

"Leadership on LGBTQ+ Equality" and requires the city leadership's commitment to fully include the LGBTQ+ community and to advocate for full equality.

It is interesting and ironic that Long Beach received a "perfect score" from HRC, even though as disclosed in a 2016 criminal trial, the Long Beach Police had been targeting gay men in public restrooms while ignoring the "lewd conduct" of heterosexuals.

Once again, it took a defendant arrested in a Long Beach public park restroom to fight back, just as Herbert Lowe and Charles Espey did.

In the case *People v. Rory Moroney*, the Long Beach Police claimed that in October 2014 an undercover officer arrested Rory Moroney, age fifty-one, in the public restroom at Recreation Park for lewd conduct and indecent exposure. Police claimed Moroney masturbated in front of the undercover officer with no other persons present. Moroney posted $10,000 in bail pending his trial. Conviction would have meant Moroney had to register for life as a sex offender.

The police testified that they had placed undercover decoy officers in the park restrooms because of complaints from residents. A review of police reports for two years did not validate there had been any complaints about that specific restroom. Records also indicated that 100 percent of the arrests for lewd conduct were made against males while complaints of heterosexual couples engaging in sex on the beach were treated differently. The defendant, Moroney, testified that the undercover officer made it clear through his eye contact and hand gestures that he was interested in Moroney.

Moroney was represented by Long Beach lesbian attorney Stephanie Loftin and Bruce Nickerson. Loftin has been defending gay men arrested in public restrooms for decades.

Loftin and Nickerson's arguments were persuasive. Los Angeles County Superior Court judge Halim Dhanidina granted the defendant's request for a motion to dismiss the charges based on "discriminatory prosecution."

The judge ruled:

By utilizing undercover officer decoys in a pre-planned, lewd conduct sting operation designed to ensnare men who engage in homosexual sex without any relationship to citizen complaints of lewd conduct at Recreation Park, the Long Beach Police Department has demonstrated its intent to discriminate against the defendant and other members of

Rory Moroney is pictured with his attorney Audrey Stephanie Loftin following the dismissal of charges and scathing ruling from the judge that the Long Beach Police Department had discriminated against gay men by targeting them in public restrooms. *From* Q Voice News.

this group. The defendant would not have been prosecuted except for this invidious discrimination.

It is this principle of equal treatment that is the cornerstone of our Constitutional democracy, the glue that binds the disparate components of society together. Our commitment to it is a necessary precondition to achieving a fair and pluralistic society.

Too often in our history has an unpopular group been made to bear the brunt of discriminatory tactics by law enforcement. The fact that members of these groups might be vulnerable to abuse requires the law to be a shield rather than a bludgeon. The arbitrary enforcement of the law as seen in this case undermines the credibility of our legal system, eroding public confidence in our ability to achieve just results. This court is determined to do its part to prevent this from occurring. In recognition of the well-established legal principles discussed herein, the court is compelled to grant the defense motion to dismiss for discriminatory prosecution.

On November 8, 2022, the day after John Lamb's birthday, Long Beach's first gay mayor Robert Garcia, onetime Republican, won election to Congress as the first gay Latino representative. Garcia replaced Alan

Lowenthal, who, from the beginning of his political career on city council, championed LGBTQ+ issues.

During Garcia's eight years as mayor of Long Beach, the city painted rainbow striped crosswalks on several streets in what it termed "the gay area" of the city. A lifeguard station painted in rainbow colors was burned down. The city restored the station and the rainbow colors. The city also facilitated several of the largest Gay Pride Parades and Festivals by attendance.

The mayor's LGBTQ+ liaison performed several times for charity in his drag queen persona. The city council named its new main library in honor of one its former residents, lesbian tennis great Billie Jean King.

Long Beach is currently planning an LGBTQ+ cultural district recognizing and supporting the LGBTQ+ community along the Broadway Corridor. This area on Broadway running between Alamitos and Junipero Avenues has long been home to a strong and active LGBTQ+ community. Many of Long Beach's gay bars and LGBTQ+ businesses are located along the corridor.

Harvey Milk Promenade Park and Equality Plaza in downtown Long Beach (212 East Third Street) opened in 2013 and is located not far from where John Lamb once lived, worshipped and was entrapped by the police, which led to his suicide.

Each year, the contributions of individuals are honored with a plaque at Equality Plaza, the centerpiece of the park that commemorates Milk and local LGBTQ+ leaders. The plaza includes a concrete replica of the soapbox on which Milk stood to inspire crowds when he spoke and a twenty-foot flagpole flying the gay pride flag. Harvey Milk Promenade Park is the first park in the nation to be named after Milk.

Just days before his assassination in 1978, Harvey Milk made a tape recording that he said should be played only if he were killed.

Milk's tape began:

> *This is Harvey Milk speaking on Friday, 18 November 1978. This tape is to be played only in the event of my death by assassination.*
>
> *I fully realize that a person who stands for what I stand for, an activist, a gay activist, becomes the target or potential target for a person who is insecure, terrified, afraid, or very disturbing.*
>
> *Knowing that I could be assassinated at any moment, at any time, I feel it's important that some people know my thoughts, and why I did what I did. Almost everything that was done was done with an eye on the gay movement.*

I cannot prevent some people from feeling angry and frustrated and mad in response to my death, but I hope they will take the frustration and madness and instead of demonstrating or anything of that type, I would hope that they would take the power and I would hope that five, ten, one hundred, a thousand would rise.

I would like to see every gay lawyer, every gay architect come out, stand up and let the world know.

That would do more to end prejudice overnight than anybody could imagine.

I urge them to do that, urge them to come out. Only that way will we start to achieve our rights.

All I ask is for the movement to continue, and if a bullet should enter my brain, let that bullet destroy every closet door.

Rest in peace, John Amos Lamb.

WHAT HAPPENED TO LOWE, WHEALTON AND OTHERS?

I t is not enough to know the details of what happened in the 1914 scandal to understand the impact it had on so many lives. It is important to learn what happened in the lives of those who knew John Amos Lamb and who were fortunate enough to live after he took his own life.

Louis N. Whealton, mayor of Long Beach

Born: October 20, 1872
Died: November 12, 1951, in Long Beach

Whealton stayed active in Long Beach issues. The new city council voted to reimburse him for the money he had paid out of pocket for the secret services used in the 1914 arrests. In 1917, Whealton helped form the Home Guard, which worked to remove all things German from the schools and the library. The Home Guard also went door to door to find Germans and make them swear their allegiance to the United States. The same year, he was personally sued by Cora Morgan for failing to pay her for her stenography work done during his secret trials of city employees. He initially won, but she was later paid by a new city council.

On September 23, 1918, Louis registered for the World War I draft.

Whealton later conducted a successful law practice at 209 Pine Avenue and represented a number of clients against the City of Long Beach.

He pushed for the use of bond money to pay for the dredging of the port to remove the silt from the Los Angeles River and was appointed to the Long Beach Harbor Commission for his efforts.

In 1918, Louis Whealton, longtime Democrat, helped form a new Republican Club of Long Beach.

In 1921, after advocating to increase Long Beach police salaries to $125 a month for patrolmen, Whealton sued the city on behalf of the businesses on Pine Avenue who wanted homeless beggars removed from the streets near their shops. Many of the "beggars" were men who had served in World War I. He also led the charge to recall William Peek, a member of the city council.

After oil was discovered in Signal Hill and Long Beach, Whealton helped form several oil companies, including the Long Beach Oil and Gas Company and the Huntington Beach Oil Company.

One of his last public efforts was to call out the city council for allowing canneries to dump fish sewage into the ocean. He claimed the stench was so strong that it caused the closure of the Hotel Virginia.

Marion Jane Lamb, sister of John Lamb

Born: August 14, 1866
Died: July 24, 1930

Marion traveled extensively after her brother's death. She moved to Redhook, New York, near her sister, where she later died. Her body was returned to California to be buried next to her brother John in Angelus-Rosedale Cemetery.

Louis Hazelwood Smith, friend of John Lamb

Born: July 7, 1879
Died: April 7, 1928, in Burbank of tuberculosis

In late 1915, Louis resumed his involvement at St. Luke's Episcopal Church and remained active for several years, helping the church form a "men's club" and serving as its vice president.

In 1916, he applied for a U.S. passport with the assistance of attorney George Hart. In his application, he stated he was "5', 11½", medium forehead, square chin, straight nose, oval face, moustache, brown/gray hair, brown eyes and ruddy complexion."

Smith said his purpose for travel was to go back to England and confer with his older brother, who was ill.

He then traveled throughout Europe in 1916 and wrote a series of articles for local newspapers about his experiences. He returned, and he and his brother Leo purchased 232 acres of "citrus land" in Temescal, near Corona, California.

The brothers sold the land in 1921 and purchased 320 acres in Salt River Valley, Arizona. He ran for Long Beach City Council in 1924 but lost to Fillmore Condit, listed as the father of the people's "Community Hospital."

Louis never married.

C.C. Cole, Long Beach chief of police

Born: 1878 in Texas
Died: 1960 in Garden Grove, California

The Long Beach City Council decided to keep Cole as chief of police after Whealton left office. He continued to be a very visible chief, forming the "peace officers' association" of policemen, constables and marshals who declared war on the "joy-rider and autothief."

Cole was also known for his unusual collection of artifacts that included "a card bearing bullets found in the desiccated bodies of United States soldiers who died on the field of the Little Big Horn river in Montana in 1876." Cole and a companion had been digging on the battlefield and reported the bodies, which were transferred to a national burial ground.

He participated in the Home Guard and pursued "rabid speakers" on the Pine Avenue Pier who made comments that were "disloyal" to the country, such as criticizing the [resident and his war policy. Cole sent plainclothes officers to mingle with the crowd and listen to the speeches and then to make arrests.

In 1918, he registered for the draft. A year later, he was pursuing "dope fiends" who frequented the Pike amusement area.

Cole was not liked by all who served in the police department, and several filed complaints against him with the city's Civil Service Commission. They alleged he misappropriated bail money taken from an arrestee and that on several occasions he interfered with the arrests of prominent citizens.

Cole was suspended from duty and resigned. During his hearing, at which he was represented by attorney Roland Swaffield, Cole's wife gave birth. He later resigned, sending a letter to the local newspaper, denying all charges. He claimed he resigned to care for his wife, who had been anxious and nervous because of the charges.

In 1920, Cole was replaced as police chief by James Butterfield, who lasted only eight months before being removed.

Cole and Butterfield were arrested in 1922 for disrupting a political gathering. They led a walkout of a meeting at the municipal auditorium after the speaker spoke against the Ku Klux Klan. The current chief of police accused Cole and Butterfield of being members of the Ku Klux Klan and then attempted to remove several officers from the police force for their Klan membership.

Cole turned his interests to real estate and sailing and bought a yacht he named *Mabel B.*

He worked in the juvenile department of the Long Beach Schools in the 1930s and received news coverage for disclosing that he was a second cousin of President William Howard Taft. That same year, he was arrested for drunk driving.

Cole wasn't heard from again until 1958, when he wrote a letter to the editor of the local newspaper, criticizing the Long Beach Police Department for placing only one patrolman per car. He died two years later at his daughter's home in Garden Grove, California.

William H. Warren, special officer who arrested John Lamb and thirty other men

Born: 1862 in Massachusetts
Died: July 20, 1915

Warren died from a self-inflicted gunshot to his heart after shooting a woman with whom he was having an affair. The account of the murder-suicide tells of an "extremely masculine" Warren, who boasted of his work to "expose" certain types of men. He claimed that in addition to his work in Long Beach he worked in New York, where he was the cause of an actor throwing himself from a window with a "trunk tied to his neck."

William "Billy" Warren became obsessed with one particular woman. He fancied himself as "a master of female hearts" and often fought with the woman, Creta Carter, whom he met while in the Los Angeles area in 1914. When she attempted to leave him, he sent a young boy to the local pawnshop to retrieve the revolver he had pawned eight months earlier. Warren and the woman quarreled, and he shot her twice and then turned the gun on himself.

The death certificate noted he was divorced from the Mrs. Warren he mentioned during the Lowe trial.

B.C. Brown, special officer who arrested John Lamb and thirty other men

No records available. News articles indicate he was fired by the Los Angeles chief of police in 1915

Reverend Benjamin Franklin K. Baker

Born: 1876
Died: 1951

Baker and his wife, Effie, traveled to Central America and Cuba in 1919. He declared he was a representative of the Studebaker Corporation and was selling automobiles and parts. The following year, he reapplied for another passport to travel to Europe representing the Commercial Research Corporation of New York. He and his wife moved to Hawaii in 1926. Records do not indicate he ever resumed ministry. Both he and his wife were cremated and are interred at East Lawn Memorial Park in Sacramento.

C.K. McClatchy, editor and publisher of Sacramento Bee *who hired a reporter in Long Beach to report on arrests of John Lamb and thirty other men*

Born: 1858
Died: 1936

McClatchy inherited the *Sacramento Bee* from his father and co-published the newspaper with his brother James. He married and had a son, Carlos, and a grandson, Charles. He retired from publishing in 1920. His great-grandson Kevin revealed in 1989 that he was gay and that his father, Charles, had been gay also.

Eugene Irving Fisher

Born: 1879
Died: 1939 of a heart attack/Buried in Riverside with other family members.

Following his reporting to C.K. McClatchy of the arrests in Long Beach, he returned to reporting for the Long Beach newspaper. In 1915, he became the secretary of the Long Beach Press Club. He was a frequent speaker at his First Baptist Church on the importance of keeping Long Beach "a dry city."

By 1918, he finished his law studies, passed the bar examination and became a member of the Long Beach Bar Association.

In 1919, he retired from the press and opened up a law practice in the National Bank Building.

Fisher became involved in local politics, campaigning for a city manager form of government to reform local politics. Because he had covered the activities of the local board of education as a reporter, he used that knowledge to run for school board. He won and was reelected several times.

In 1927, Fisher pushed the school board to support the establishment of a junior college, which resulted in Long Beach City College. His focus was to provide pre-vocational and vocational programs beyond high school. He left the school board in 1931. He died of a stroke in 1939.

Charles E. Espey

Born: 1869
Died: 1957

Espey died at the Los Angeles County hospital. His occupation was listed as "real estate salesman."

Things did not go well for Espey after his trial. In 1917, his house was foreclosed on. His wife, Olivia, however, remained active in the Daughters of the American Revolution and the Woman's Christian Temperance Union.

He and his family moved to a newer house, where his wife continued to entertain the members of her clubs. Espey volunteered as a precinct worker during local elections. His wife, Olivia, died in 1931.

Herbert Lowe

Born: July 2, 1879
Died: June 10, 1936

Lowe died in Long Beach from heart problems. His death certificate indicated his wife, Louise, had divorced him.

After the trial, life went back to "normal" for Herbert Lowe. He immediately began traveling and reporting to the local newspapers of his excursions. In 1915, he drove to San Francisco and brought back a number of specimens of a "new sweet-pea with exceptionally long stems" for display in the front windows of his shop.

In 1917, he took his mother on a six-week automobile trip across the United States and then back to Detroit, where he purchased a 1918 Buick touring automobile and drove it home to Long Beach.

Herbert added several "stunning new designs" to his floral shop, including an electric fountain with colored lights and colored water. The fountain was adjacent to a fishpond and another fountain installed in his shop.

He registered for the draft in 1918 and opened an additional florist shop in Long Beach.

His mother, Julia, died in 1924. She had transformed a five-acre tract near what afterward became Bixby Park into Long Beach's first commercial nursery. The Alamitos Nursery provided the plants and flowers for the Lowe's Florist Shop.

That same year, he boarded the steamer *Buford* and sailed to the South Seas on what he described as a "fairy dream" trip. The *Long Beach Magazine* featured several pages concerning Lowe's trip and his impressions of the islands.

He continued his travel and while in Europe became acutely ill. Upon returning, he told the newspaper, "There is no place like Long Beach." Never once did the local press mention his arrest and trial.

From time to time, Lowe would travel to expand his collection of shells. His work was so extensive that the Smithsonian Institution and other museums consulted him.

He willed his shell collection to the San Diego Society of Natural History, along with a maintenance fund of $25,000.

When he died, not one word was printed about his 1914 arrest and trial.

Judge Joseph J. Hart

Born: February 4, 1845
Died: December 20, 1929

Hart was a member of the first city council in Long Beach. He had formerly served in the Union army during the Civil War.

After serving as Police Court judge for nine years, he lost his reelection in 1915 even though the law firm of Swaffield & Swaffield took out an advertisement endorsing Hart for reelection.

A strenuous campaign was waged against him for his conduct in the cases of Lamb and Espey.

Two years later, he was sued for false imprisonment of a man arrested for allowing his fourteen-year-old son to drive his automobile. The jury found against Hart, who was fined fifty dollars.

Hart stayed active in his church, Immanuel Baptist, and in the Pioneers Club, serving as its president for several years.

His wife, Agnes, died in 1921.

Roland G. Swaffield

Born: January 7, 1884
Died: February 15, 1961

After the trials, Roland served as an army captain in the 23rd Company Coast Artillery Coast Artillery in San Pedro for one year during World War I. He continued taking controversial cases against the City of Long Beach and on its behalf.

Swaffield is credited as having won a lawsuit against the State of California, giving Long Beach the rights to the tidelands and the oil underneath.

St. Luke's Episcopal Church, Long Beach, California

The church, which began as a mission in Long Beach in 1897 with services being held in the Long Beach Masonic Hall, continues to be a popular and active congregation. Its members work on a number of social justice issues and the congregation is considered to be one of the most welcoming of the LGBTQ+ community.

The church was rebuilt in 1917 at Atlantic Avenue and Seventh Street from funds realized with the sale of the former location to the First Christian Church. On October 18, 1917, the granite cornerstone for the new church and sanctuary was laid on Atlantic Avenue under one corner of the one-hundred-foot tower. A number of documents were placed inside.

The congregation grew, and in 1930 the St. Luke's Choristers of Long Beach, California, were organized with sixty men and boys by William Ripley Dorr. The group appeared in several movies and were popular nationally. The church services at which they performed were broadcast weekly on the local KFOX radio station.

In 1933, Long Beach was hit by an earthquake, which caused considerable damage to the spire and other parts of the church. More than $40,000 was raised nationally for its repair.

Reflecting on the history of the church, Long Beach historian Walter Case wrote in the October 13, 1933 *Long Beach Sun* a portion of a historical sketch of the church:

> *Any group picture of the early workers of our little mission on the shore would include the following names: the W.S. Stephens family, the Harnett family, the J.W. Tucker family, the Ayles family, the Lamb family and others that may come to mind.*

Each year, a contingency of church members marches in the Pride Parade. Clergy and vestry conduct a Communion on the Bluff at the start of the parade.

Unitarian Universalist Church of Long Beach

By 1922, a building at 850 Lime had become the home of the church. With a growing membership, a new building was constructed in 1957 at its current location, 5450 Atherton. The church was shared with the Southern Baptists for two years.

The Long Beach Church installed its first female pastor in 1934, Reverend Cora Van Velsor Lambert.

Over the years, the Unitarian Church became a sanctuary and housed refugees. The church history notes: "This was a daring act when few other UU congregations answered the call to house political refugees who feared life-threatening repression and persecution."

Today, the church is LGBTQ+/TGQNB affirming, hosts Days of Observance and participates in the Pride Parade.

BIBLIOGRAPHY

1. Knowing the Precise Amount of Poison

Hyatt, W.H. *Henning's General Laws of California: As Amended and In Force at the Close of the Forty-Third Session of the Legislature, 1919, Including Initiative and Referendum Acts Adopted at the General Election of 1920*. San Francisco: Bender-Moss Company, 1921.

Kansas City Star. "She Is the First Electrician. Mrs. Iva Tutt Owns the Plant and Furnishes the Light for Long Beach." December 11, 1898.

Long Beach Telegram and Daily News. "Lifeless Body Found On Rocks. At Pt. Firmin [*sic*] with Empty Cyanide Vial Nearby—Leaves Scribbled Note to Sister." November 14, 1914.

2. What Brought People to Long Beach

California Immigrant Union and the Inducements to Settle There. San Francisco: California Immigrant Union, 1871.

California South of Tehachapi. San Francisco: Southern Pacific Company, 1904.

Case, Walter. "You Know That? E.C. Denio Wrote Bill for Property's Return." *Long Beach Sun*, March 23, 1942.

"Field Notes of a Cemetery Traveler." *Park and Cemetery and Landscape Gardening*, March 1921.

Frank, Rochelle. "History in the Streets." *Southland Magazine*, January 5, 1964.

Long Beach Press Telegram and Daily News. "Pioneer Long Beach Woman Passes to Eternal Rest. Death Claims Mrs. Belle McKee Lowe, One of City's First Settlers and Active in Its Development." April 9, 1918.

————. "Where Roses Are in Bloom. Where Summer Is Perpetual and Where Any Possible Monotony Is Ever Relieved by New Beauties and an Every-Day Sunshine That Is Electrifying and Life-Giving Long Beach—Queen of Beaches—The City by the Sea, S. Townsend Predicts Population of 50,000 for Long Beach by 1920." December 30, 1910.

Long Beach Sun. "Old Time Residents May Form a Club." August 2, 1933.

————. "Pioneer Rites Are Arranged. Mrs. Orlena Healey Came to the City in 1882." October 20, 1933.

Los Angeles Evening Post-Record. "New Long Beach Lines. Nearly Swamped by Eager Crowds." July 4, 1902.

Sixty Years in California a History of Events and Life in California Personal Political and Military Under the Mexican Regime During the Quasi Military Government of the Territory by the United States and after the Admission of the State into the Union Being a Compilation by a Witness of the Events Described by William Heath Davis Known as Kanaka Davis a Half Breed. San Francisco: A. Leary Publisher, 1889.

Wells, Drury, and Audrey Wells. *California Tourist Guide and Handbook Authentic Description of Routes of Travel and Points of Interest in California*. Berkeley, CA: Western Guidebook Company, 1913.

3. *John Amos Lamb: Pharmacist, Dedicated Churchman and Banker*

Long Beach Evening Tribune. "Ten Pages—Stick of Pitch Makes Dirty Smear on Fair Name and Fame of Long Beach—Mayor Eno and Trustee Losee Arrested Last Night for Bribery." December 30, 1905.

Long Beach Press. "Organization. Completed and St. Luke's Episcopal Mission Has Become a Parish. Articles Adopted at Annual Meeting in the Church Last Night—An Important Step Was Taken." February 3, 1905.

Long Beach Telegram and Daily News. "Threats Made Against Mayor Disfigurement for Life Is Among Them." January 18, 1905.

Long Beach Tribune. "For Greater Long Beach Terminal Island and East San Pedro Link Fortunes with City That Does Things—Despite the Efforts of Jealous San Pedro Annexation Carries by Small Majority and Long

Beach Can Now Proudly Refer to Our Fine Harbor and Breakwaters—Yesterday's Vote." August 17, 1905.

Magoffin, Frank H. "John A. Lamb Died Victim Bogus Detectives' Trick: Innocent Man Arrested." *San Bernardino Daily Sun*, November 20, 1914.

San Bernardino County Sun. "Personal." August 12, 1902.

Scranton Reporter. "Hotel Collapsed. Four Men Killed. Four Others Fatally Injured and About a Dozen Missing in Long Beach, Cal., Accident. Construction Faulty." November 10, 1906.

4. John Lamb and Louis Hazelwood Smith: The Once Inseparable Couple

Daily Telegram. "Minor Mention." December 2, 1907.

Long Beach Press. "Good Fortune Comes to Parish. Two Thousand Dollars Given by Heirs of the Crocker Estate Unique Story of the Gift Is Interestingly Told by Vestryman J.A. Lamb." February 6, 1906.

Long Beach Telegram and Daily News. August 31, 1914.

———. "Full Fledged Citizen." May 21, 1914.

———. "Old Residents of Long Beach Permanently Organized at First Dinner and Meeting in Hotel Virginia Arrange Annual Event. Reminiscences of Old Days Feature First Pioneer Rally. Judge Hart Named as Permanent Head of Organization." May 9, 1914.

———. "Saint Luke's Honor Rev. and Mrs. Bode. Occasion Tenth Wedding Anniversary of Popular Episcopal Rector and His Wife." June 2, 1914.

5. Louis Napoleon Whealton: A Tammany Hall Reject

Long Beach Telegram and Daily News. "Fusionists Resort to Desperate Methods Disregard Pertinent Questions of Policy and Revive Old Tactics of Personal Abuse." November 10, 1913.

———. "Glorious Wind-Up of Whealton Campaign Crowd of 4,000 People Cheer Mayoralty Candidate to Echo Significant Tribute to Popular Man." November 11, 1913.

———. "Independent Progressive Party. The Executive Committee. 'Why We Endorse Mr. Louis N. Whealton For Mayor.'" November 5, 1913.

———. "Office on Ticket Universal Demand for Changed Conditions Forcefully Expressed at Polls." December 3, 1913.

————. "The Serpents Tongue and the Dreamer Craig's Swan Song and Humphreys' Record Treated in the Address of Louis N. Whealton at the Forum Oct. 30th 1913." November 1, 1913.

————. "Whealton Answers Attacks of Fusionists Mayoralty Candidate Addresses Big Audience at Alamitos School and Minces No Words." November 7, 1913.

————. "Whealton Elected by a Splendid Majority by Over 1000 Votes for Mayoralty. Four Councilmen Chosen, and Three Are Yet to Be Elected. Congratulations All Around." November 12, 1913.

Press-Telegram. "Realty Board Enjoys Animated Discussion of Woman's Suffrage Press Bureau Head of Repartee with Few Retorts Courteous Los Angeles Antis Opens Debate. Miss Martin's Position Is Vigorously Assailed by Mere Man. Lawyer Whealton Ladies' Champion." October 4, 1911.

————. "What About the Telegram's Candidate for Mayor? Authorized Advertisement. Paid by W.R. Shively Who Is He? Where Is He? Who Are His Friends?" October 28, 1913.

6. Whealton Conducts Secret Trials Against City Staff

Long Beach Telegram and Daily News. "An Unfortunate Condition." January 3, 1914.

————. "Library Commission's Formal Statement Relative to the Matter of Miss Ellis' Resignation and Events Which Led to Its Presentation." March 20, 1914.

————. "Library's Commission Formal Statement." March 20, 1914.

————. "Sowing Dragon's Teeth." July 6, 1914.

Los Angeles Times. "Mayor Accuses Police; Dozen Warrants Issued." April 18, 1914.

————. "Sensation. Get What You Can. Signed, Whealton." June 24, 1914.

————. "Why? Please Make Them Shut Up. Whealton Appeals to Grand Jury Against Press. Would Have Budd-Morgan Case Facts Suppressed." June 25, 1914.

Press-Telegram. "Bob O'Rourke Resigns as Captain." May 27, 1914.

————. "Editorial. Long Beach As Dry Town." July 10, 1914.

————. "Hizzoner Is One Fine Actor. Starts Raids on Eve of Election." April 18, 1914.

————. "Mayor Whealton Talks at Forum." April 18, 1914.

————. "Vague Hints at Fight Against Miss Ellis. Mayor Whealton Reiterates Charge That Probe Will Estrange Her Friends." March 14, 1914.

7. Whealton Finds Scheme to Replace Drained City Secret Services Fund

Long Beach Telegram and Daily News. "The Deadly Parallel. The First Unitarian Church and the Whealton Campaign." November 11, 1913.

————. "Flag Day Celebration." June 3, 1913.

————. "Says That He Is Innocent. Long Beach Pastor Arrested on 'Suspicion.'" October 10, 1913.

Los Angeles Herald. "Plea for Jonquil Girls Sounded in 'Mary Magdalene.'" October 1, 1913.

Press-Telegram. "Jury Acquits on First Ballot. George H. Bixby Not Guilty of Contributing to the Delinquency of a Minor." September 30, 1913.

Sacramento Bee. "Little by Little the People Will Believe." January 7, 1915.

————. "Need of State Legislation Against a Horrible Vice." December 21, 1914.

————. "Upon the Question of True Californians." March 15, 1915.

8. The State of Sodomy

Appeal to Reason (Kansas). "Degeneracy of Capitalism. They Who Denounce Socialism Discovered in Act of Sodomy in Many Places." December 21, 1912.

C.K. McClatchy and Eugene Fisher file, Center for Sacramento History, December 5, 1914.

C.K. McClatchy and Eugene Fisher file, Center for Sacramento History, November 20, 1914.

Cobb, Rodney, and Irma West. *In Good Times and in Bad: The Story of Sacramento's Unitarians 1868–1984.* Sacramento, CA: 2008.

East Oregonian. "Male Garbed Woman Is Given Her Freedom." November 24, 1911.

Johnson, Lewis, Jr. *Advice to Boys: With Information They Ought to and Must Know. Their Make-Up, Dangers, Traps that Catch Men.* N.p., 1900.

Lawrence Daily Journal. "Presbyterians Are Gay." February 3, 1899.

Long Beach Telegram and Daily News. "Asserts His Innocence. Dr. Baker Granted Vacation to Prepare Defense." October 11, 1913.

———. "Available Money for Site." September 15, 1913.

———. "Praise Words for Sermon." July 18, 1913.

Los Angeles Times. "LB Recital of Shameless Men." November 19, 1914.

Modesto Bee. "Remarkable Career of Women Ends in Death." December 28, 1922.

Monrovia Daily News. "Republican Mass Meetings Held at Women's Hall." October 23, 1914.

Press-Telegram. "Dr. Baker Heads Band Concert Movement." July 9, 1913.

Sacramento Bee. "Lowe Case Calls Attention to Need for a Law." December 23, 1914.

9. Long Beach Launches Public Comfort Station

Long Beach Press. "Comfort Stations Now Open for City." June 27, 1912.

———. "Parks, Parking on Bluff and Comfort Station Up on a Bond Issue." August 19, 1910.

———. "Proposed Public Comfort Station, Beautiful Design. Interior Finish Is Planned in White Marble." August 11, 1910.

Long Beach Telegram and Daily News. "Ordinance 590. Salaries of Janitor and Janitress." August 17, 1912.

———. "Remarkable Growth in Population and Advance in Civic Improvement Is Noted." May 26, 1911.

———. "Some Radical Alterations. And Changes Recommended in Public Comfort Stations." January 9, 1915.

News-Pilot. "Sixty Days in Jail for Degenerate Defacing Ladies Comfort Station." September 22, 1914.

"Public Comfort Station, New York City Hall, Chicago." *Engineering Review*, 1912.

10. Lamb's Fateful Stroll Along the Walk of a Thousand Lights

C.K. McClatchy and Eugene Fisher file, Center for Sacramento History, December 5, 1914.

Homo History. "Seeing Red in the 1900s." http://www.homohistory.com.

Long Beach Press. "Ground Broken For $15,000 Open-Air Studio by Balboa Amusement Producing Actors." December 11, 1913.

———. "Rogers to Fly Hither on Sunday." December 9, 1911.

Long Beach Telegram and Daily News. "Advertisement. An Adequate Auditorium." September 22, 1914.

———. "Auditorium Disaster Kills 30!" May 24, 1913.

———. "Boston Theater." September 26, 1914.

———. "Countless Multitude Greets Arrival of Fleet." April 20, 1908.

Press-Telegram. "Easter Celebrations in the City." April 20, 1908.

San Bernardino County Sun. "John A. Lamb Died Victim Bogus Detectives' Tricks; Innocent Man Arrested." November 20, 1914.

11. Eugene Irving Fisher: Long Beach Reporter Feeds Details to Sacramento Bee

C.K. McClatchy and Eugene Fisher file, Center for Sacramento History, 1914.

Long Beach Press. "Freeholder Candidate Meeting." March 17, 1914.

———. "News Boys' Club Is Latest Feature of Uplift Work by Local Y.M.C. Association." May 27, 1914.

———. "Newsboys License." November 7, 1913.

———. "Old Residents of Long Beach Permanently Organized at First Dinner and Meeting in Hotel Virginia Arrange Annual Event." May 9, 1914.

Los Angeles Times. "Long Beach Uncovers 'Social Vagrant' Clan." November 14, 1914.

San Francisco Call. "Eugene I. Fisher Who Was Made Modesto Freeholder." August 2, 1910.

12. Herbert Lowe Trial Releases Details of "Special Officers" Entrapping Local Men

Long Beach Telegram and Daily News. "College Women's Club." June 21, 1912.

———. "Mr. Herbert Lowe, the Florist Has Returned." May 8, 1908.

———. "Scientific Expedition." April 2, 1912.

Strong, A.M., and E.M. Chace. "Herbert Nelson Lowe" *Nautilus* 50, no. 1 (1936): 64–66.

13. Los Angeles Times *Publishes Details and Names of Arrested Long Beach Social Vagrants*

Long Beach Press. "News Boys' Club Is Latest Feature of Uplift Work by Local Y.M.C. Association." May 27, 1914.
———. "Newsboys License." November 7, 1913.
Los Angeles Times. "Long Beach Uncovers 'Social Vagrant' Clan." November 14, 1914.

14. Only One Newspaper Prints Lamb's Entire Suicide Note

C.K. McClatchy and Eugene Fisher file, Center for Sacramento History, 1914.
Long Beach Press. "Slays Self on Reading 'Expose.'" November 14, 1914.
Long Beach Telegram and Daily News. "John A. Lamb Suicides in Fit of Despondency. Lifeless Body Found on Rocks. At Point Firmin [*sic*] with Empty Cyanide Vial Nearby—Leaves Scribbled Note to Sister." November 14, 1914.
———. "Short News Items of Local Interest. Funeral Services for John A. Lamb." November 17, 1914.
Los Angeles Times. "Takes His Life Through Shame. Death Note Asserts Innocence but Unprovable. Churchman's Suicide Adds Sensation to Case. Long Beach Scandalized by Police Court Expose." November 15, 1914.
Sacramento Bee. "Vast Scandal in Los Angeles Is Reported as Suppressed." November 18, 1914.
San Bernardino County Sun. "Bogus Detectives' Trick; Innocent Man Arrested." November 20, 1914.
San Pedro News-Pilot. "Suicide at Point Fermin from Scandal, John Lamb Takes Poison Following Newspaper Exposure of Fine. Prominent Man in Long Beach Circles. Strange Tale of 'Social Vagrant' Clan Denied in Note to Sister." November 14, 1914.

15. Gender Impersonation Is All the Rage in Long Beach

C.K. McClatchy and Eugene Fisher file, Center for Sacramento History, 1914.

Frost, Natasha. "The Early 20th-Century ID Cards That Kept Trans People Safe From Harassment: The Radical Days of the Weimar Republic, Just Before the Rise of Nazism." *Atlas Obscura*, November 2, 2017.

Long Beach Telegram and Daily News. "Amusements. Boston Theater." September 25, 1914.

———. "Bentley Grand." February 13, 1913.

———. "Midsummer Fashions Make First Bow on Stage." June 27, 1914.

Los Angeles Times. "Special Prosecutor to Press Vice Case." November 18, 1914.

Pomona Daily Review. "Getaway Quick Interviews." November 18, 1914.

Sacramento Bee. "Exposure of Bizarre Orgies Causes Suicide Unable to Bear Shame, Wealthy Church Member of Long Beach Talles Poison—Thirty Men Fined or Sentenced—Participants in Orgies Dressed as Women in Kimonos." November 14, 1914.

Ullman, Sharon R. "'The Twentieth Century Way': Female Impersonation and Sexual Practice in Turn-of-the-Century America." *Journal of the History of Sexuality* 5, no. 4 (1995): 573–600.

16. *Long Beach Ministers Outraged by Lamb Suicide, Demand Publisher Stops Brutal Journalism*

Los Angeles Evening Express. "Monstrous Journalism." November 19, 1914.

Los Angeles Times. "Another Trial in Long Beach." December 2, 1914.

———. "Defense of Degenerates." December 3, 1914.

———. "Good Authority. Holy Bible on the Sodomites. Sins of Gomorrah Like Those Exposed at Long Beach. 'Brutal Journalism' in Old and New Testaments God's Denunciations of Violators of His Law." November 26, 1914.

———. "Long Beach. Pay for Seats; Trial Delayed. 'Social Vagrant' Case Held Up; Juror Ill. Chief Witnesses for State 'Mysteriously Gone.' Are They Hiding in Fear of Convicted Men?" November 17, 1914.

———. "Order in the Court." November 24, 1914.

———. "Ouch! Clean-Up Just Begun. Spooners on the Sands to Follow the Grist of 'Social Vagrants'—Parson Mason Starts Something, Too. Police Judge Hart Declares for Full Publicity—Committee That Doesn't Come to 'The Times.'" November 22, 1914.

Otis, H.G. "Cleaning Up Long Beach." *Los Angeles Times*, November 21, 1914.

Regan, Colleen. "Women Jurors in California: Recognizing a Right of Citizenship." *California Supreme Court Historical Society Review* (Fall/Winter 2020): 2–9. https://www.cschs.org.

Sacramento Bee. "Publicity Is Needed; And Then More Publicity." November 23, 1914.

17. *Herbert Lowe Wins and Other Named Social Vagrant Demands Trial*

Los Angeles Times. "Attorney Aims Blow at Detective Witness. Officers Prevent Fracas in Second Trial of Long Beach Social Vagrancy Case—Justice Hurries Testimony Along to Get It Over With—Issue Raised Over Purity Campaigns." December 11, 1914.

———. "Blackmail Is His Defense. Man Accused of Degeneracy Counters Attack, His Testimony Sensation of Vagrancy Cases. Prominent Men on Stand to Uphold Character." December 23, 1914.

———. "Father Broken Hearted." December 27, 1914.

———. "Jury Acquits in Six-O-Six. Long Beach Florist Freed of Hideous Charge. Stool-Pigeons and Police Given No Credence. One Conviction in Three Years Is Court Record." December 12, 1914.

———. "LB Recital of Shameless Men." November 19, 1914.

———. "No Criminal Intent." February 13, 1895.

18. Sacramento Bee *and* Los Angeles Times *Taunt Long Beach Over Holy City Image*

"In re Application of Clarence Lockett for a Writ of Habeas Corpus." Supreme Court of California, January 9, 1919, 179 Cal 581 (CA 1919) Crim. No. 2215. Crim. No. 2220, January 9, 1919.

Sacramento Bee. "Bee's Publicity Light on Great Vice of Day Shows Need of Punitive Measures Although Half Cannot Be Old, Enough Has Been Said to Show Extent of Vicious Practices of Men, Who Work Both in Light and in the Dark." December 24, 1914.

Sacramento Star. "Rev. Franklin Baker Arrested as 'Vag' Well-known Here." October 10, 1913.

19. Whealton Fights New Form of City Government

Long Beach Telegram and Daily News. "City Clerk Riley Elopes at Midnight with New Charter." January 6, 1915.

Press-Telegram. "Anti-Charter Petition Is Written. Long Threatened Attack on Ballot—Verdict of City's Electorate at Last Comes to Focus. Mayor Whealton and S. Alexander So-Called Initiative Is Believed Impotent Even Though It Should Be Put Through." December 29, 1914.

———. "Big Guns Boom at Monument Unveiling." July 3, 1915.

———. "Charter Foes Win More Recruits. Ballot Verdict Reported Today by Leader S. Alexander. Mayor Whealton Advisory Chief Speculation on Outcome Unprecedented Attempt to Kill Election by Simple Petition." December 30, 1914.

20. Arrestee Sues for Being Slandered During Stories on Long Beach

Long Beach Telegram and Daily News. "Julian Eltinge at Hoyt's December 8th. Will Be Only Date in Southern California." November 21, 1919.

Los Angeles Times. "Long Beach Figures in Hot Libel Suit." October 27, 1916.

———. "Verdict for Defendant." October 28, 1916.

Press-Telegram. "She's a Man, No He's a Girl. Well, It's Eltinge." December 4, 1919.

21. The Final Trial on 1914 Scandal

Earl v. Times-Mirror Company. Supreme Court of California, February 25, 1921, 185 CAL 165 (CAL 1921).

Los Angeles Evening Express. "Anderson Shows Malice Actuated Times." November 28, 1916.

———. "Edwin T. Earl Wins $30,000 Verdict for Libel." November 28, 1916.

———. "Times Vilification Was Underhand Blow at Press, Claim." November 25, 1916.

22. Long Beach Continues Targeting Gay Men in Public Restrooms Until 2016

City of Long Beach. "10th Year Anniversary Harvey Milk Promenade Park Equality Plaza Induction Ceremony." https://www.longbeach.gov.

Daily News. "Homo Nest Raided. Queen Bees Are Stinging Mad." July 6, 1969.

Desert Sun. "Long Beach Gay-Pride Parade May Instead Be Protest March." June 11, 1985.

Equality California. "Long Beach Mayor Robert Garcia Makes History as First Openly LGBTQ+ Immigrant Elected to Congress." November 18, 2022. https://www.eqca.org.

Human Rights Campaign. "Municipal Equality Index." https://www.hrc.org.

Independent. "Headlines, Stories Mustn't Stray Beyond the Facts." August 21, 1977.

———. "Raid Lewd Show Here." September 13, 1955.

International Imperial Court. https://lbimperialcourt.org.

KCAL News. "Judge: Long Beach Police Targeted Gays In Sting Operations." April 30, 2016.

LGBTQ Center Long Beach. https://www.centerlb.org/mission-history.

Los Angeles Times. "Ballots 2-Vote Victory." April 19, 1992.

———. "Local Elections." May 29, 2006.

———. "Long Beach Councilman Censured over Comments About Gays and Lesbians." October 6, 1993.

———. "Long Beach Councilman Resigns over Partnership." February 8, 2006.

———. "Long Beach Feels Effects of Anti-Gay Speech." September 1, 1996.

———. "Women's Studies Foes Sue to Halt Cal State Program." July 25, 1985.

Mattachine papers. One Archives at the USC Libraries.

News-Pilot. "Mailer." March 23, 1996.

New York Times. "Milk Left a Tape for Release If He Were Slain." November 28, 1978.

Press-Telegram. "Choo-Choo Train Man." November 7, 1960.

———. "Homosexual 'Guild' Aims to Better Police Relations." April 24, 1977.

———. "Homosexuality Rife at Beaches, Parks." July 29, 1977.

———. "Neighborhood Bar Stars on Videotape." July 9, 1977.

———. "Sojourner Offers Books and Place to Rap." December 16, 1974.

Robeson, George. "Southend Is Home For Homosexuals." *Press-Telegram*, August 18, 1966.

Shilts, Randy. *The Mayor of Castro Street*. New York: St. Martin's, 1982.

Statement of Decision People v. Moroney. Superior Court of California County of Los Angeles. April 29, 2016https://static1.squarespace.com/static/55774bb0e4b013bae3b7e863/t/57317e76c6fc085da9e1d1de/1462861435734/Statement+of+Decision+-People+v+Moroney.pdf.

Zonkel, Phillip. "Halim Dhanidina Discusses Long Beach Lewd Conduct Ruling." QVoice News, September 8, 2022.

23. What Happened to Lowe, Whealton and Others?

Cobb, Rodney, and Irma West. *In Good Times and in Bad: The Story of Sacramento's Unitarians 1868–1984*. Sacramento, CA: 2008.

Congregational History. https://www.uuclb.org/about-us/congregational-history.

Long Beach Sun. "Herbert Lowe Funeral Rites Set For Friday. Retired Florist Noted Shell Collector Dies in Sleep." June 11, 1936.

———. "Unitarians Will Install New Pastor Tomorrow." February 24, 1934.

Long Beach Telegram and Daily News. "Election Endorsements." May 11, 1924.

———. "Manager Suspend McClendon in Klan Row." November 8, 1922.

Los Angeles Evening Express. "Murder, Suicide Tragic Verdict." July 21, 1915.

Press-Telegram. "London During War Times Described by Long Beach Man Just Home from Trip. Louis Hazelwood Smith Has Some Exciting Experiences but Escaped Submarines and Zeppelins in Visit Abroad." May 20, 1916.

———. "More Charges Are Filed in Chief Cole Complaint." August 14, 1919.

———. "Observations and Viewpoints." March 29, 1927.

———. "Voluminous Petition Filed by Whealton." January 25, 1921.

San Bernardino Sun. "Miss Marion Lamb." July 29, 1930.

San Francisco Examiner. "Gays Making Their Presence Felt." June 7, 1989.

ABOUT THE AUTHOR

G errie Schipske is passionate about the history of her hometown, Long Beach, California. Born in the U.S. Naval Hospital, she later earned degrees in history, legislative affairs, nursing and law. She worked as an intelligence clerk with the Central Intelligence Agency, staffed a member of Congress, served as the City of Long Beach's first public information officer and then pursued careers in law, healthcare, education and politics.

Gerrie is the first lesbian to be elected to public office in Long Beach—winning three times. She and her spouse, Flo Pickett, have been together since 1980, raising three children and a granddaughter and spoiling their dog, English.

Also by Gerrie Schipske

LGBTQ+ Long Beach
Rosie the Riveter in Long Beach
Early Long Beach
Early Aviation in Long Beach
Historic Cemeteries of Long Beach
Historic Hospitals of Long Beach
Suffragettes of Early Long Beach
Remarkable Women of Long Beach
The Case of the Missing Librarian (historical fiction)

Visit us at
www.historypress.com